THE HISTORY OF WORLD TEAMTENNIS:

Over Forty Years of Courting Equality

Benjamin Snyder

Foreword by Billie Jean King and Ilana Kloss

Archway Publishing books may be ordered through booksellers or by contacting:

Archway Publishing
1663 Liberty Drive
Bloomington, IN 47403
www.archwaypublishing.com
1 (888) 242-5904

Because of the dynamic nature of the Internet, any web addresses or links contained in this book may have changed since publication and may no longer be valid. The views expressed in this work are solely those of the author and do not necessarily reflect the views of the publisher, and the publisher hereby disclaims any responsibility for them.

Any people depicted in stock imagery provided by Thinkstock are models, and such images are being used for illustrative purposes only. Certain stock imagery © Thinkstock.

ISBN: 978-1-4808-3777-5 (sc)
ISBN: 978-1-4808-3779-9 (hc)
ISBN: 978-1-4808-3778-2 (e)

Library of Congress Control Number: 2016916272

Printed in the USA.

Archway Publishing rev. date: 04/25/2017

Contents

About the Cover v

Foreword by Billie Jean King vii

Foreword by Ilana Kloss ix

Introduction: Celebrating the League's 40th Season (2015) xi

Chapter One: Seasons One to Five (1974-1978): 1

    Highlight #1: Larry King: The WTT Mastermind 16

Chapter Two: Seasons Six to Ten (1981-1985): 22

    Highlight #2: Billie Jean King Takes the Reins 31

Chapter Three: Seasons Eleven to Fifteen (1986-1990): 35

    Highlight #3: WTT Rec League takes tennis to the people 40

Chapter Four: Seasons Sixteen to Twenty (1991-1995): 47

    Highlight #4: Martina Navratilova and Jimmy Connors Join 51

Chapter Five: Seasons Twenty-One to Twenty-Five (1996-2000): 62

    Highlight #5: Welcoming the Williams Sisters 70

Chapter Six: Seasons Twenty-Six to Thirty (2001-2005): 74

    Highlight #6: Ilana Kloss Takes Charge as CEO......................................78

Chapter Seven: Seasons Thirty-One to Thirty-Five (2006-2010):..................89

    Highlight #7: World TeamTennis and the USTA Partnership 101

Chapter Eight: Seasons Thirty-Six to Forty (2011-2015): 110

    Highlight #8: The Magic behind the Kastles 117

Chapter Nine: Season Forty-One and Beyond: 129

Chapter Ten: Fun Facts from 40 Years of WTT 133

WTT Championship Teams from the League's History 139

League Innovations and Firsts..150

World TeamTennis Awards (1974-2016) 158

Acknowledgements 166

About the Cover

The watercolor rendition of the King Trophy that adorns this book's cover was painted by Janet Nunn and commissioned by Billie Jean King. Nunn discussed her influence for the painting as well as the process she used to paint in an interview for this book.

Janet said that King gave her photographs to work off of initially and that it was a difficult image to copy at first.

"I worked on the trophy and by the time I got it painted and then got the reflections, that was really a lot of work," she said.

When she finished the first rendition, however, she realized she needed to do more with it to make the King Trophy come to life (and bring forward World TeamTennis' unique imprint). "It needed more texture," she explained. "I know this is kind of weird, but the texture of it is what made the whole thing."

So, she enjoyed a well-earned night's rest when inspiration suddenly struck in the morning. "I picked it up at like five o'clock in the morning and said this is how you do this," she said.

And then she realized she was in the zone, sort of like in tennis. "You're in tune with everything and art's the same way, but I do remember it being an all-day adventure," said Nunn. "It went by really quick."

"You have to have breaks, but sometimes you are just so so focused that you lose all track of time and I think it's been fifteen or twenty minutes, but I might have been there for two hours, and not even know that it was two hours' worth of time," she said.

She explained that she was wary at first trying to paint the image based on what King commissioned versus her own interpretation. "I was kind of nervous at first but then I thought that I'll just keep trying until I get it right," said Nunn. "I didn't know if I could be on the same thought process—what [King] was thinking. A lot of times when you have someone look at an image that you have, you're thinking one thing and the other person is thinking a whole completely different thing."

"What I tried to capture is that feeling of winning the trophy because that's what the trophy is all about," Nunn continued. "But the hardest part is to make sure that what you're thinking in terms of winning on paper is very similar to what Billie is thinking."

Nunn discussed how there are times when it can be difficult getting inspired to paint, similar to an athlete competing on court. "There are days you're going, 'Oh, my goodness, why am I doing this?' and then there are other days when it just works," she said. "Everything just works for you; and you're thinking, 'I can't do a bad job.'"

She had that experience with this piece in the end. "It's kind of like hitting a great shot," said Nunn.

Janet Nunn Watercolors
www.janetnunnwatercolors.com/

Billie Jean King and Ilana Kloss have led World TeamTennis over the last 40 years. Photo Credit: World TeamTennis

Foreword by Billie Jean King

If you have ever seen a World TeamTennis match, you have seen my philosophy of life in action – men and women – all genders – competing on the same team, making equal contributions, working together toward a common goal.

And that's what I want the world to look like.

As a child I loved team sports and I played basketball and softball before picking up a tennis racquet. And that love for being part of a team is what lead to the development of the WTT concept and format.

I was honored to be the first draft pick of the League in 1974 and that was definitely one of the highlights of my career.

The inaugural WTT season in 1974 was full of excitement and one of my favorite memories of playing that year with the Philadelphia Freedoms was when Elton John would sit on our team bench in full uniform and cheer us on. When Elton wrote his smash hit "Philadelphia Freedom" to honor me and the team, it not only was the perfect signature song for a sports team, it also was a great gift to the people of Philadelphia.

Sitting on the bench with your team is one of the greatest experiences for any athlete and WTT is no different. The conversations and observations from the bench are part strategic, part conversational and usually therapeutic. Over the years, I was blessed to be on the bench with some great teammates and many of those friendships and relationships remain strong today.

As a player I loved the tension and the drama of the WTT competition and format and I know it made me a better player. I vividly remember one match with the New York Apples in 1977 against the Cleveland Nets that had us all on the edge of our seats. Mixed doubles was the final set and Ray Ruffels and I were locked in a tight match against Wendy Turnbull (at least I think it was Wendy!) and Marty Riessen. We were playing in a venue with a low ceiling and at six-all in the final set Supertiebreaker – with the match on the line with the next point – I walked over to Ray and said, be ready for anything because I may hit a lob right over Marty's head. Ray looked at me like I was from outer space! I threaded the needle with an offensive lob and we won the match.

And it just doesn't get any better than that.

I am also proud of how we have expanded the WTT format beyond professional tennis and thankful for the thousands of recreational players and league directors who play and run WTT leagues around the globe. The use of our format at major junior tournaments like the WTT Junior Nationals, at the Tennis on Campus college club program and at a wide variety of tennis events is proof people enjoy playing the WTT format and we love having them in our family.

Tennis has been my platform and the sport has given me so many opportunities in my life. WTT has been a very big part of that enjoyment. I love being part of a team and I will forever believe in WTT. It's good for the sport and it's been really good for me.

At World TeamTennis it really takes a strong team to put on this great sports experience night after night, year after year. We have been blessed to have many of the world's greatest players compete in WTT and honored to be part of so many strong communities.

We wouldn't be here without the co-founders who shared my vision for World TeamTennis – Larry King, Fred Barman, Frank Fuhrer, Jordon Kaiser and Dennis Murphy.

The team owners and their staffs – from the past and present members of the military who present the color guard at matches to the countless volunteers who staff each venue – are committed to producing quality entertaining events each and every night. The professionals at the WTT league office – especially our CEO (and a former WTT player and coach herself) Ilana Kloss – are the backbone of the organization that runs our League year-round.

And our fans are simply the best in the sport. Thank you all for your involvement, your commitment and your dedication and I am so happy we are on the same team!

Billie Jean King
World TeamTennis Co-Founder

Foreword by Ilana Kloss

"Follow your dreams."

I heard those words from Billie Jean King when she took time to hit a few tennis balls with me when I was just an 11-year-old ball girl at a pro tournament in my hometown of Johannesburg, South Africa. From that moment on, it was clear to me that my dream was to become a professional tennis player, even though at the time it would be years before the women's tour would get started.

My dream became a reality when I was drafted to play the first season of World TeamTennis in 1974. I was now on a professional tennis team alongside the best players in the world. It's been more than four decades but I have never forgotten the magnitude of that moment or any of the numerous memories of my more than 40-year involvement with World TeamTennis.

At the time, playing tennis professionally seemed like the culmination of a dream but it was really just the beginning – the beginning of a life-changing journey. I've been fortunate to have many great experiences in my tennis career, but there was always something special about being part of the World TeamTennis family.

As a player, it was the intensity and high level of competition. The shared joy in our victories and the painful defeats turning teammates into lifelong friends.

As a coach, it was the thrill of mentoring players and leading a team to the WTT championship.

As an executive, my experience has been from a different vantage point but it's been equally rewarding to form partnerships with passionate team owners, sponsors and several generations of players who have also loved the WTT experience.

The true unsung heroes and sheroes of our sport are the League and team staffs, along with community leaders and volunteers, who are all tirelessly dedicated to promoting World TeamTennis.

There have been many challenges along the way but there have be so many more high points – from visiting with the President at the White House with our championship team to making sports history as only the fifth U.S. pro sports league to reach the 40th season milestone (joining good company in the NFL, NBA, MLB and NFL).

I'm proud of the way we have elevated tennis with our extraordinary platform of gender equality, innovation and access. Our teams, players, fans and sponsors have bought in to our brand of tennis.

Along the way, we challenged the sport with a number of firsts and innovations – from instant replay to multi-colored courts to names on the back of players' shirts to Supertiebreakers to fans keeping balls hit into the stands. The list goes on. Many of our firsts have been adopted by others, but our drive to continue to innovate and showcase team tennis is as strong as ever.

More than anything else, I am most proud of what WTT stands for and what it represents to the next generation. You have to see it to be it, and WTT is a great example of that. WTT is about both men and women competing together on a level playing field and contributing equally to the team. It's about our vision to grow tennis and make it a true team sport. It's about providing a level of access and involvement fans generally can't get with other sports. It's about giving communities a sense of ownership in tennis and a connection to our players. It's about bringing the best professional players to local communities where kids can see them working together as a team. And that's an important inspirational message.

World TeamTennis has been such an integral part of my life. As a young child I dreamed of playing tennis professionally, making a difference and most importantly, doing what I loved. WTT has given me all of that and so much more.

I hope you enjoy this journey through the first 40 seasons as much as I have . . . there's much more to come.

Ilana Kloss
Mylan WTT CEO/Commissioner

Introduction: Celebrating the League's 40th Season (2015)

Since its inception in 1974, World TeamTennis has captured the hearts of thousands of fans each year who clamor to watch some of the world's great tennis stars play together as a team in intimate settings across the United States.

For young fans, the access at a WTT match simply cannot be beat. Want an autograph from Serena Williams? You got it. Did John Isner's monster serve or an Andre Agassi return slam into the stands? Also fair game.

The league's signature multicolored court sets the tone visually; a World TeamTennis match is unlike any other in the world.

"The most fun thing for me is that the fans get to talk and shout and scream and cheer and interact right through the event," explained Leander Paes, a player with the Washington Kastles who claimed his sixth title with the team in 2015 during the league's historic 40th season.

"That's the fun thing. The interaction between the players and the fans is key for me for tennis in the way that we market the game. The music that comes and the colored courts—that's another thing that I really like."

Then there's David Macpherson, a former WTT and ATP (Association of Tennis Professionals) player and former coach to Bob and Mike Bryan, the doubles phenoms from the United States. He's been a convert to the format for years. "It's a special kind of energy, coming together as a team, which you don't get to do on the regular tour. Bringing four players together—two men, two women, for five events and playing for a city," he said. "It's just got so many special characteristics that go into it."

"To have the home city support you and bring that energy to the matches every night?" Macpherson added, "There's just nothing like it."

The league prides itself on fostering competition, fun, excitement, and, of course, equality each time WTT players hit the court. After all, the league's co-founder Billie Jean King fought hard both during her professional career as the world's top tennis player and as the winner of thirty-nine Grand Slam titles in singles and doubles to ensure that women were equal to men both on the court—and off it. In fact, co-founder King's push for the female professional tour ultimately led to the creation of the Women's Tennis Association.

She took that same passion for bringing equality to sports, and, as a result, to mankind through her love of World TeamTennis, beginning with its first season in 1974. Needless to say, she never looked back. And that equality has transcended the sports league to this day.

How so? A WTT match, as many have considered it, serves as a microcosm for an ideal society. Men and woman team up together toward a common goal, i.e., winning a match. Through WTT, tennis becomes much more than a group of franchises who seek to claim the King Trophy at the end of a three-week season (or months-long season, as in the past). Instead, they're in it together, and there's the opportunity to impact the lives of children throughout the United States by giving them access to professional-quality matches that they would otherwise have had little opportunity to watch in person.

And as is the case with Smash Hits (WTT's annual charity event held with Sir Elton John and featuring tennis legends such as Andre Agassi, Stefanie Graf, Andy Roddick, John McEnroe, Pete Sampras, Jimmy Connors, Martina Navratilova, Serena Williams, Venus Williams, Lindsay Davenport, Chris Evert and more), there's also a historic commitment to bettering the community—and the world.

But on an even more intimate level, the WTT format is enjoyed by all genders around the globe for which tennis plays a huge role in shaping their lives.

Since 1986, WTT has held a robust recreational league including for all ages in partnership with the United States Tennis Association. It's been enjoyed by thousands around the country starting from when the league began this branch of its operations.

***

Since WTT kicked off in 1974, there have been a plethora of highlights, from players making breakthroughs to innovative rules and strategies employed by the athletes. New relationships formed between coaches and athletes to take back to the ATP and WTA tours, and even a few careers restarted, such as in the cases of Martina Hingis, Kim Clijsters, and Jimmy Connors.

Budding tennis stars have the league to thank for their careers blossoming: look no further than American champion Andy Roddick, or up-and-coming Madison Keys, who was coached by former WTT MVP and world No. 1 Lindsay Davenport, or Taylor Fritz. A young Serena and Venus Williams, two of the greatest female athletes in history, played WTT, too. As did others who committed to the league not only because of their passion for the sport of tennis, but also because they believed in (and, of course, still believe in) the work of Billie Jean King and of Ilana Kloss, who has served as CEO of the league since 2001. Together, the duo have grown the league since its early days and subsequent hiatus to ensure that WTT remains part of tennis' rich past, present, and future.

In honor of the league's 40th season, WTT players over the years were given the opportunity to talk about what playing as part of Billie Jean King's legacy meant.

"First of all, I loved WTT so much," said Chris Evert, who played during the league's formative years for the Phoenix Racquets in 1976 and 1977 as well as the Los Angeles Strings in 1978. Among the tennis accolades she collected, including being the No. 1-ranked player in the world, Evert also captured a WTT crown with the Strings.

Chris Evert, who won 18 major singles titles during her career, played World TeamTennis during its first years. Photo: World TeamTennis

Additionally, she was honored as Female MVP in 1976 and 1977, Female Rookie of the Year in 1976, Playoff MVP in 1978, and Women's Singles scoring leader in 1976 and 1978.

But while Evert highly regarded her professional career aside from WTT, she relished the chance to play on a team with the league. "Tennis is such a self-absorbed and isolated sport. In WTT, you get on a team and have people rooting for you," she added.

Evert even attributed her success at Wimbledon in 1976 to her time spent playing WTT, thanks to the coaching she received from Tony Roche. "You get to play singles, doubles, and mixed and get free coaching. I had two different kinds of coaching," she explained. "I had Tony Roche. In 1976, I won both Wimbledon singles and doubles. He taught me how to play doubles."

Evert added, with laughter, "And then two years later, I had Ilie Nastase for a coach and he didn't show up for practice."

Notably, Evert also enjoyed huge drawing power whenever she played. After all, she was one of the most popular American tennis players to pick up a racquet at the time. In a *New York Times* article from 1976, the author and coach Roche discussed the player's ability to get fans excited about the league and the sport. "Miss Evert is the leading gate attraction in the league. Large crowds come to see her wherever she plays," according to the newspaper. "She drew 7,709 fans to the Nassau Coliseum on Wednesday, and in Phoenix, the Racquets average nearly 8,000 fans a match."

"I played in this league for three years, and I didn't see 7,000 people come to see me play," said Roche to the *Times*. "When I see 7,000 people, I know they're there to see Chris."

The American is just one of many of tennis' greatest players to have a fruitful WTT career. Take Paes as another example of a player grateful for the chance to play in a team-oriented tennis league. Not only that, but he considers WTT as a family away from home.

"I'm very blessed to be a part of it in my own little way and to create my own little history coming from India into Washington, DC, to create a second home for myself there," he said.

"To every single person who has been a part of WTT over these 40 years, a big happy birthday, a happy anniversary, and a real congratulations for a fabulous 40 years that I've been able to partake in," he added. "It's been a wonderful ride."

British player Virginia Wade, who competed with the league for the New York Sets in 1974, 1975, and 1976, as well as with the New York Apples in 1977 and the Golden Gaters in 1978, also lauded her experience. "Well, I have to say that although it was very hard work because you were doing a lot of traveling and moving around from one place to another, when you were actually on the court, it was so stimulating, so exciting, and it was wonderful to have a team around you that supported you," she explained. "Plus the fact that we had magnificent coaching and practice, so we all improved as players."

Then there are the Bryan brothers, two of the best doubles players to ever compete in the sport of men's doubles, who have also taken part in WTT matches for a number of franchises during their careers. "Doubles is extremely important in Mylan WTT. It's a majority of the match, which is great for us and for doubles," said Mike Bryan. "You're never out of it. It seems like it always comes down to the wire."

He added: "You see all types of tennis. It's fast-paced. We get out there and bring our energy right from the first point. You have to get it done for the team. We take great pride in winning most of our matches in TeamTennis. We have a great time putting on a show for the fans and winning for our city, owner, and team."

Those experiences likely mirrored the ones felt by the players who competed during the 40th season in 2015. The league celebrated its legacy across the country through involvement by some of the top tennis stars in the world, along with a thrilling season that saw the Washington Kastles claim its fifth consecutive title, a league first, by defeating the upstart rival Austin Aces in a nail-biter of a championship match.

***

A capacity crowd gathered in Washington, D.C., at Kastles Stadium, which is located at the Smith Center. It's a cavernous space with WTT's signature funky-colored court, alerting fans that they're about to witness a tennis match unlike no other. And for sure, that's exactly what the match between the two top teams of the season all but ensured on their way to the Mylan WTT Finals. After all, on one side of the net were the four-time consecutive champions, the Kastles, owned by Mark Ein and coached by the gregarious Murphy Jensen. On the other side? The Austin Aces, owned by Lorne Abony and coached by five-time doubles major title winner Rick Leach.

The scene was set after a powerful season, illustrative of the league's 40 seasons. All eyes were on the Washington Kastles to claim yet another title, given their dominance over the past few years. In fact, they had won five titles in just six years. They were gunning for another and, of course, meant business. The team comprised some of the world's top talent in tennis, too. The player captain? Leander Paes, a stalwart Kastles player and easily one of history's best doubles players. As the Kastles competed in the 2015 season for a shot at the King Trophy once again, Paes held an astounding nine men's major doubles titles, along with eight mixed doubles major titles (notably, he would go on to win a ninth with teammate Martina Hingis at the US Open just a month later).

"Well, tennis is a great vehicle to bring in community and bridge people from all different walks of life and from different cultures and from different backgrounds," said Paes as he was heading into the season. "The whole concept of World TeamTennis that Billie Jean King and a whole team have come together and put together is phenomenal."

"I am coming into my seventh year to play World TeamTennis for the Washington Kastles. It's such a thrill to go out there and honor Billie Jean King, honor the game of tennis, honor Mark Ein, my boss at the Washington Kastles. And to play for a team and a community that has become home to me," he added, noting his success having played six seasons and winning league titles an astonishing five times. "And to go out into my seventh season as the captain of the team and entertain our fans in Washington and bring them a bit of happiness through a hard day when they finish their day's work is just a thrill for me."

For the historic 40th season of the league, the Indian celebrity and star athlete was joined by one particularly successful player: legend and tennis tactician Martina Hingis. The "Swiss Miss," (as she was known as she claimed titles at a young age in her prime), held 18 major titles to her name in singles, doubles, and mixed doubles. She also enjoyed a resurgence in recent years thanks in large part to her WTT play. With her doubles prowess, she proved time and again her effortless ability to clutch key matches for her teammates. The ability to do so with the Kastles was no different.

Paes spoke highly of his mixed doubles partner with the Kastles and of his opportunities to partner with some of tennis' greats along the way. "It's a great opportunity when you get the chance to play with champions. With the Kastles, I've gotten the chance to play with Serena Williams, Venus Williams, Victoria Azarenka, and Rennae Stubbs, and now Martina Hingis," he said. "I've had a great chance to play with all these greats of the game who have won singles Grand Slams, doubles Grand Slams, and mixed doubles Grand Slams."

Paes continued: "That's the beauty of World TeamTennis, you've got men and women mixing together playing singles, doubles, mixed and quick sets, and it's very exciting. And that's the fun about World TeamTennis, we all come together to showcase the game of tennis."

More specifically, Paes lauded his partnership with Hingis, which has helped the Kastles become so dominant in doubles events since the Swiss player joined the team for the 2013 season. "I think it's our understanding of the game. I think it's our understanding of the space on the court," he said. "And it's also our deep friendship."

"Martina is a great champion, and all of you have watched her on the screens and read about her in the newspapers and magazines, and you'll know the champion she is as a tennis player," Paes added. "For me I know her as the champion she is as a human being, and that's what makes it special. I've always got her back."

He continued: "When we get out onto the tennis court, or even if we're off the tennis court, the friendship that I share with Martina is something really special. Playing with her on the Washington Kastles is what built that camaraderie on court, that then we carried out onto the Australian Open where we won the whole Australian Open Grand Slam without losing a set."

And joining veterans Paes and Hingis: a familiar name in American tennis, Venus Williams, a member of the WTT Ownership Group, a seven-time major singles winner and champion for equality on court, including equal prize money. Venus, who played in WTT for 11 seasons up to the 40th, also won four League titles, including for the Philadelphia Freedoms in 2006, along with the Washington Kastles in 2011, 2012, and 2014.

Perennial top-ranked Sam Querrey from the United States and Anastasia Rodionova rounded out the squad. Rodionova, whose sister Arina has also played for the Kastles in 2011 and 2012, talked about her experience with the team. "Well, when I sat on that bench, when I just came to watch my sister play, I told Mark that if I ever am back playing World TeamTennis, this is the only team I'm going to be playing for," she said. "There I was one year later, playing with my sister on the team."

She discussed the atmosphere at Kastles matches as well as the audience. "The fans were amazing, the crowd was really into getting in to watch. And it's not only about the crowd, it's how players interact with each other," said Rodionova, a Kastles player during their winning seasons in 2012, 2013, and 2014. "You really have that team environment on the bench and that felt really good, and I really wanted to try it myself."

Rodionova also competed during the season with substitutes Madison Brengle (who would go on to playing a large role in the Mylan WTT Finals), Denis Kudla, and Rajeev Ram.

The Kastles saw a rivalry brew with the Austin Aces from nearly the get-go of the year, which kicked off in July. Indeed, the Aces, owned by Lorne Abony, may have been in existence for just two seasons, but they quickly proved their ability during the regular season. And the team jived well together, despite an early exit from hometown hero Andy Roddick.

Although the 2003 US Open men's singles champion ultimately proved unable to compete due to injury, the WTT veteran was joined by a group of talented teammates. Teymuraz Gabashvili of Russia was the team's male singles player, having achieved a career-high heading into the season with a ranking of No. 52 in singles earlier that year. As the No. 2 Russian male singles player, he's been friends with teammate Alla Kudryavtseva.

"I'm really excited because I know another on the team, Alla," he revealed ahead of the season. "She's my friend. So, I'm really excited." Gabashvili, who advanced to the fourth round of the French Open once, added that playing in WTT is "kind of different than the ATP Tour. We will see how it goes. It's tough to say, I've never played it."

Ultimately, he'd get used to the format—and thrived, too, including a win over Andy Murray of Britain a few weeks after the season ended.

Kudryavtseva, who has a WTA Tour singles title and eight doubles titles, reached a career-high ranking of No. 56. "I think I'm an aggressive player. I fight," she said. "I love the atmosphere when people are pumped and I get pumped and this kind of drive; it's what we play the game for."

That, she added, would help her ahead of the 2015 season. "And I think World TeamTennis provides that, and I'm looking forward to playing in Texas because I've never been there actually, and I've traveled America for so long and I've lived here awhile," she explained. "Texas just avoided me, so I'm just going to go and embrace the culture."

Joining the two Russians? Jarmere Jenkins, Elina Svitolina and Nicole Gibbs on the line-up.

Gibbs, a 2012 All-American at Stanford who reached a career-high ranking of No. 89, appeared pumped by the prospect of playing with the Aces during the 40th season, as did her teammates. "I think the atmosphere that World TeamTennis brings is really unique obviously. The courts are super fun," she said, speaking about the transformative quality of the league. "I think the format is really engaging for the fans, shortened sets, no ad. I think that makes a really exciting environment, brings the fans really intense games and points. I think it's a really great fan experience for the game of tennis."

Adding to that was Billie Jean King's legacy for equal rights. "I'm so excited to be part of Billie Jean King's vision for World TeamTennis. She's obviously had such an impact on the sport, from college tennis all the way to professional tennis with equal prize money," said Gibbs ahead of the season. She said being involved gives her the ability to strive for more in her own career in terms of fighting for equal rights.

"And I think the more that I can be involved in the things that she's tried to accomplish on tour, the better for me as a female athlete and really gain connections with the history of tennis," said Gibbs.

***

With the line-ups for the two teams set during the annual draft ceremony earlier in the year, the celebration for the 40th season kicked off at Indian Wells. "I think we're very adaptable. We've been able to adjust to the changing of the generations to give fans what they want," said Ilana Kloss, the CEO of WTT since 2001, and a former No. 1 in doubles, at the onset.

At Indian Wells, Kloss continued to hype the historic 40th season and discussed the opportunities for the fans and teams going forward during the summer months. "When you're on the court, you're really focused a lot on yourself; in this role, I think we really look to the outside world, and really want to provide something special for communities," she said. "WTT is all about access, and we are an unbelievable platform to provide that in local communities and also on a national basis."

She continued: "We're still relevant in our 40th season. Kids and fans still love the product, love pulling for their team, and I think it's really great that tennis has a team element where you can come and cheer for your city and be truly part of the team sports landscape."

Kloss said the 40th season marked just the beginning of the league: "Every day I feel really lucky to be doing something that I love and know, and only hope that the next 40 are as good as the past 40."

The enthusiasm ahead of the season's start cemented it in place for a hard-fought run by the teams involved, which comprised the Western Conference teams with the Aces, the California Dream, the San Diego Aviators, and the Springfield Lasers. In the Eastern Conference with the Kastles were the Philadelphia Freedoms and the Boston Lobsters.

***

To begin, the Kastles played the Lobsters, who were coached by former WTT player Jan-Michael Gambill. The team included a mix of talent from the U.S. and abroad, including Scott Lipsky, Irina Falconi, Arantxa Parra Santonja, Chase Buchanan and Alex Kuznetsov. They were to compete on their home court at the Manchester Athletic Club. But on that day, the Kastles would prove too strong for the Lobsters, claiming a tight 20-17 win as the league's defending champions.

Meanwhile, the Aces played their first match the next day—Monday, July 13—to start their 2015 campaign, and just their second season in history after a 2014 debut with lackluster results. Like the Kastles, they'd take out the Lobsters in another close call: 20-18.

The match featured dominant performance for the Aces in men's and women's singles, but tight sets in women's doubles, mixed doubles, and men's doubles.

Things came to a head soon after between the Aces and Kastles when they played their first match against one another soon after. The match was contested at Kastles Stadium at the Smith Center and featured marquee player Venus Williams.

A tight first set in men's singles saw the match get off to a close start. "There was a beloved American legend playing in front of a packed crowd, a timeless doubles star flying in straight from Wimbledon, a hometown hero surrounded by family and friends, and a fan favorite returning to the house he helped build," an article about the match read on the Kastles' website.

"All that was missing was the win," it continued.

The match report added: "Venus Williams played her part, defeating Nicole Gibbs 5-2 in singles. Leander Paes showed off spectacular volleys for the 3,125 fans in attendance. Arlington (Va.) native Denis Kudla defeated World No. 52 Teymuraz Gabashvili 5-4 in the opening set. And former Kastles closer Bobby Reynolds served as the honorary assistant coach."

"Bashing balls from the baseline and moving briskly, Kudla jumped ahead 3-0 in the following game, earning four set points," according to the match report. "Gabashvili, however, found his return in time to save all four. He followed with a hold for 4-4, forcing a tiebreaker."

It continued: "Gabashvili claimed the first point of the tiebreaker with a return winner, but momentum wasn't done switching hands. Kudla won five points in a row to the delight of his D.C. fans, sealing the set when Gabashvili netted a forehand."

The Kastles ultimately pulled through, winning 5-4. But then the Aces showed their newfound form after a lackluster first season in 2014, taking both women's doubles and men's doubles in dominant fashion to bring their match score to 14-9, a score calculated by the total number of games won in the WTT match after three events.

While the Kastles surged to a lead with Venus Williams in tow for women's singles, her victory wouldn't be enough. Mixed doubles proved to be the decider, with Williams and Leander Paes succumbing to the Aces 5-3 to lose the match 22 games to 17 in just over two hours.

The Kastles' loss was just their third in 34 home matches dating to the 2010 season and was a fascinating example of the surging play from the Aces that would come to mark the new season as theirs to lose.

As the season continued, the Kastles and Aces proved to be two of the strongest in the league. They built off those early victories and ended up with a vice grip on their respective conferences.

After their July 14 contest, both teams proved dominant in their matches. On July 18, for instance, the Kastles routed the Philadelphia Freedoms in one of the most lopsided matches for the season, winning 23-6. In fact, it was the largest margin of victory in Kastles history, an article on the team's web site proclaimed.

Per the Kastles: "After the Freedoms took the first set 5-3, Kudla and Brengle were on court to win 20 of the next 21 games, including 16 in a row. The end result was a 23-6 Washington win with the improbable score line of 3-5, 5-1, 5-0, 5-0, 5-0." In fact, losing six games "are the fewest a Kastles opponent has ever scored and the 17-game margin of victory matches the largest wins in eight of years of Kastles tennis."

The team succumbed just eight games, in beating Boston 25-8 on July 9, 2014, and when it defeated Kansas City 25-8 on July 22, 2012.

By July 22, the Aces were on a roll by capturing a perfect 8-0 in match play. But before the Kastles and the Aces went against one another for the second time, the teams would lose less than a handful of matches each during the next nearly 10 days. They were dominant ahead of their second clash on July 24 at the Gregory Gymnasium at the University of Texas, the home stadium for the Aces.

In that match, the season was well underway with the Conference championships looming ever closer in the distance. In fact, the winner of the match would help the Kastles clinch a playoff spot in the Eastern Conference.

The Kastles were a new team when they played against the Aces in a rematch. They started strong in mixed doubles, with legends Hingis and Paes partnering up for success. After all, they beat the formidable team of Alla Kudryavtseva and Teymuraz Gabashvili 5-3 with relative ease, at least by the scoreboard.

Soon after, Hingis took to the court in the next set for women's doubles, putting on a display of tactical prowess that saw her rise in the WTA doubles rankings that year. Partnering with Anastasia Rodionova, they defeated Nicole Gibbs and Kudryavtseva in a 5-1 rout.

While Gibbs proved too strong for Rodionova in women's singles with a 5-2 victory, men's doubles and men's singles both went the way of the Kastles. The team from D.C. ended up claiming a 22-14 victory to clinch the top seed in the Eastern Conference and to get one step closer to hoisting the King Trophy for a sixth time in seven years.

With the 40th season coming to a crescendo, the last few teams were left to fight for the crown. In the Eastern Conference, the Kastles defeated the Boston Lobsters to take them out of contention in the Eastern Conference.

"With home court advantage safely secured, the Kastles played the role of playoff spoiler Wednesday, preventing the Boston Lobsters from a postseason berth with a 22-14 win.

Boston's loss was Philadelphia's gain as the Freedoms found themselves in an Eastern Conference Championship rematch with the Kastles the next night.

The match played out in exciting fashion, too. One night after losing 10 of 11 games in singles to the Austin Aces, the Kastles won 10 of 11 singles games courtesy of Martina Hingis and Sam Querrey, beating Boston for the 18th straight time dating back to July 22, 2010.

It would be Sam Querrey who would help secure the victory, too. "Querrey began the match in men's doubles, which featured strong Kastles serves and surprising volleys by Lobsters substitute Christian Harrison," an article noted. "Querrey hit an ace in each of his two service games, and Leander Paes added one of his own as Washington held four times with ease."

Harrison would be a factor in the match, although he couldn't force a tiebreak in the men's double set after all. "However, when Harrison served at 3-4 in the set and 3-1 in the game, the young American was unable to force a tiebreaker—Washington stealing the set 5-3 with a backhand return winner from Querrey," according to the article.

So with the Kastles in contention for the year-end title once again and the Lobsters out, the Eastern Conference took place between the Washington D.C. team and the Philadelphia Freedoms. The match, like their previous contests over the 40th season, was another lopsided affair. In fact, the Kastles won 24-9 in another dominant performance.

"By sweeping Philadelphia, the Kastles improved to 11-0 all-time in the postseason and earned their most lopsided playoff win ever," according to a write-up.

Meanwhile, Anastasia Rodionova, the top women's doubles player for the season, was recognized as the 2015 WTT co-female MVP, along with Anabel Medina Garrigues of the California Dream from the Western Conference.

But Rodionova wasn't alone in her distinction over the years. Rodionova was congratulated by the three other Kastles to be named Most Valuable Player: Leander Paes (2009 & 2011), Martina Hingis (2013), and Bobby Reynolds (2012).

The match started off strong for the Kastles, too. "Paes and Hingis, the Wimbledon and Australian Open champions, got things off to an ideal start. The Kastles lost all three of their mixed doubles sets to the Freedoms during the regular season, but that was without Hingis in the lineup," it continued. "Washington went on to win the game, and the set 5-1, when Hingis won a rapid volley exchange at the net over Townsend."

With the Kastles dominating and getting closer to another berth in the finals, frustration began boiling over for the Freedoms in men's doubles. "Though Robby Ginepri managed to hold and even the set, Paes quickly made it 2-1 on his serve before working more magic at the net," according to the article. "He hit a pair of rapid volleys to steal the first two points on Melo's serve, then generously accepted two volley errors from the Freedoms that gave Washington a 3-1 advantage."

Querrey's big-serving got a 4-1 lead for the Kastles, although Ginepri ended up claiming a game. "The Freedoms would not win another as Paes served the set out with an overhead into Melo's leg, a half-volley winner down the line, and a service winner that the French Open champion Melo frustratingly forehanded over the Kastles' team bench," according to the match report.

Querrey's serving was an asset in men's singles when he beat compatriot Ginepri 5-0 to clinch the win.

"Playing with Leander is always a thrill," said Hingis after the win. "We just know each other's games so well, and we click when we have to. We started off strong to help get the team going."

"It's so much fun to play in this setting here," Querrey said. "For the most part, I've been playing in the last spot, and my teammates have done a great job in giving me a big lead. It's allowed me to play freely."

By returning to the finals, "the Kastles were aiming to become the first team in the 40-season history of Mylan WTT to win five straight King Trophies, having joined the 1997-2000 Sacramento Capitals with their 2014 triumph," according to a WTT article. "The Kastles were also looking to equal the Capitals mark of six overall championships."

***

The Western Conference championship round, meanwhile, was played by the Aces and the California Dream. Like in the Eastern Conference championship, the Aces claimed their rightful place in the finals with relative ease. They beat the Dream 25-14 to set up their sport against the Kastles in just their second year in existence after boasting an exceptional 12-2 regular season.

But the match pitting the Aces against the team from California didn't start smoothly by any means. The culprit: flight delays and weather problems, which actually caused the California Dream to arrive in Austin 80 minutes after the scheduled start time.

"The first ball was hit at 9:43 p.m. (central) as the top two mixed doubles teams in the league faced off. Austin got on the board first by holding serve and never looked back," according to a match report.

As the match wore on, the Aces translated their success during the regular season in a winning combination in the Western Conference championship round. "Alla Kudryavtseva's forehand winner down the line broke Anabel Medina Garrigues' serve in the fourth game to put Austin up by a 3-1 margin," according to a match report. "Kudryavtseva and Teymuraz Gabashvili teamed up for a victory over the league's top-ranked tandem of Neal Skupski and Garrigues to give the Aces an early 5-2 lead."

The Aces pulled away in women's doubles and men's doubles for a 15-9 lead during half-time. "Gajdosova, who finished the regular season as the top-ranked player in women's singles, faced world No. 20 Svitolina in the fourth set. Gajdosova couldn't hold serve in the fourth game and Svitolina rolled to a 5-1 set win," the article added. "In men's singles, Gabashvili was challenged in men's singles by Sandgren, who fought until the end for his team. Gabashvili asserted himself in the tiebreaker, delivering a scorching running forehand winner before sealing the Aces victory shortly after midnight with his sixth ace of the match."

"It was amazing. I didn't have a lot of pressure because my team did fantastically," said Gabashvili after the match. "We found our energy and showed our best. I am feeling great on the court."

Austin's coach, Rick Leach, also had positive words to say about his team's work during the match. "I am happy with the way our team fought and came together when we needed to," he said.

***

And with that, the dream final for the 40th season was set: the Washington Kastles against the up-and-coming Austin Aces. The match was to be decided at Kastles Stadium in Washington, DC, and whoever won would be making history. For the Kastles, it was another title to add to their treasure trove and brimming collection—a chance to get even with the Sacramento Capitals, who mustered up six titles during the '90s.

Meanwhile, the Aces were looking for glory for the first time in World TeamTennis history.

The stadium was packed at the onset of the match; the atmosphere was created by the fans, who were palpably excited for the momentous occasion. "Washington was in control of the highly-anticipated matchup between the top two teams in the regular season from the start," an article about the match stated.

"In the opening set of mixed doubles, Teymuraz Gabashvili and Alla Kudryavtseva reeled off four straight points to win the first game," but it wasn't to last much longer as Paes and Hingis picked up their game.

But the Kastles would race to a fine start, illustrating their experience over the nervous Aces. "Paes held serve to even up the match at 1-1. Martina Hingis hit a winner down the middle to break Kudryavtseva's serve to go up 2-1. Hingis held to give Washington a 3-1 lead before Gabashvili brought the Aces back to 2-3 with a huge service game."

The article added, "Paes held serve then the Kastles got another critical break of Kudryavtseva's serve to close out the first set, 5-2."

The Kastles had the top-ranked women's doubles team in the league with Anastasia Rodionova and Hingis solidifying their team's strong play by grabbing a 2-0 lead. Although the Aces did get on board and broke Rodionova's serve, Washington snatched a 5-4 win to claim a 10-6 lead.

"Washington seemingly took control of the match in men's doubles with an early break of serve to go up 2-1. The Kastles took a 4-2 lead on a Sam Querrey ace. Washington closed out the set 5-3 to take a commanding six-game lead at halftime, 15-9," according to the WTT article about the match.

"Querrey continued his strong play in men's singles with a 5-4 win over Gabashvili, the top men's singles player in the league, to give Washington a 20-13 edge going into the final set of women's singles," it continued.

In 2015, the Washington Kastles won a record fifth consecutive World TeamTennis title, their sixth overall championship. Pictured (l. to r.): Madison Brengle, coach Murphy Jensen, Martina Hingis, owner Mark Ein, Sam Querrey, Leander Paes and Anastasia Rodionova.
Photo: CameraworkUSA

The King Trophy was in sight for the Kastles yet again. All that was standing in the way was a match between Madison Brengle and the Aces' No. 20, Elina Svitolina.

Svitolina was handed the task of bringing Austin back from a seven-game deficit against Madison Brengle. "Svitolina, who beat Brengle 5-1 in their only previous Mylan WTT meeting, looked in control early on before a controversial call going against the Kastles ignited the Washington crowd," explained the article.

Immediately, Svitolina fell behind a break, although later broke back in the next game. The pressure mounted on Brengle, as Svitolina claimed the set 5-3 to take the match into extended play.

But the American played some strong tennis, punctuating the win with a backhand winner to take the match, 24-18, and ending the 40th season for the sixth overall championship win for the Kastles.

That victory brought the Kastles even with the Sacramento Capitals' collection of six titles dating back to 2007.

Captain Leander Paes was named the Finals MVP and lauded his team's performance afterward. "It's just a beautiful moment to share," Paes said. "I've had a really long career and done some really special things, and this is way up there with the best of them."

"I'd like to dedicate this MVP award to every single Kastles member, not only on the court but behind the scenes and every single Kastles fan," he said.

"It's a dream come true," said Murphy Jensen, the Kastles' coach through their six victories over the years. "It's so different, you'd think this'd get old hat, but it doesn't. It was a bigger challenge because players were coming and going during the season, but to get them all to perform the way they did against an extremely tough team says a lot about our organization."

Chapter One: Seasons One to Five (1974-1978):

The Formative Years

1974 TEAMS & PLAYERS:
EASTERN DIVISION
Atlantic Section

Baltimore Banners:	Byron Bertram, Don Candy, Bob Carmichael, Jimmy Connors, Ian Crookenden, Joyce Hume, Kathy Kuykendall, Jaidip Mukerjea, Audrey Morse, Betty Stove.
Boston Lobsters:	Pat Bostrom, Doug Crawford, Kerry Melville, Janet Newberry, Raz Reid, Francis Taylor, Roger Taylor, Ion Tiriac, Andrea Volkos, Stephan Warboys.
New York Sets:	Fiorella Bonicelli, Carol Graebner, Ceci Martinez, Sandy Mayer, Charlie Owens, Nikki Pilic, Manuel Santana, Gene Scott, Pam Teeguarden, Virginia Wade, Sharon Walsh.
Philadelphia Freedoms:	Julie Anthony, Brian Fairlie, Tory Fretz, Billie Jean King, Kathy Kuykendall, Buster Mottram, Fred Stolle. COACH: Billie Jean King

Central Section

Cleveland Nets:	Peaches Bartkowicz, Laura DuPont, Clark Graebner, Nancy Gunter, Ray Moore, Cliff Richey, Pat Thomas, Winnie Wooldridge.
Detroit Loves:	Mary Ann Beattie, Rosie Casals, Phil Dent, Pat Faulkner, Kerry Harris, Butch Seewagen, Lendward Simpson, Allan Stone.
Pittsburgh Triangles:	Gerald Battrick, Laura DuPont, Isabel Fernandez, Vitas Gerulaitis, Evonne Goolagong, Peggy Michel, Ken Rosewall. COACH: Ken Rosewall
Toronto/Buffalo Royals:	Mike Estep, Ian Fletcher, Tom Okker, Jan O'Neill, Wendy Overton, Laura Rossouw.

WESTERN DIVISION
Gulf Plains Section

Chicago Aces:	Butch Buchholz, Barbara Downs, Sue Eastman, Marcie Louie, Ray Ruffels, Sue Stap, Graham Stilwell, Kim Warwick, Janet Young.
Florida Flamingos:	Mike Belkin, Maria Esther Bueno, Mark Cox, Cliff Drysdale, Lynn Epstein, Donna Fales, Frank Froehling, Donna Ganz, Bettyann Stuart.

Houston EZ Riders:	Bill Bowrey, Lesley Bowrey, Cynthia Doerner, Peter Doerner, Helen Gourlay-Cawley, Karen Krantzcke, Bob McKinley, John Newcombe, Dick Stockton.
Minnesota Buckskins:	Owen Davidson, Ann Hayden Jones, Bob Hewitt, Terry Holladay, Bill Lloyd, Mona Guerrant, Wendy Turnbull.

Pacific Section

Denver Racquets:	Jeff Austin, Pam Austin, Francoise Durr, Stephanie Johnson, Kristien Kemmer Shaw, Andrew Pattison, Tony Roche. COACH: Tony Roche
Golden Gaters:	Dick Bohrnstedt, Barbara Downs, Roy Emerson, Lesley Hunt, Ilana Kloss, Frew McMillan, Whitney Reed, Denise Triolo.
Hawaii Leis:	Butch Buchholz, Ross Case, Brigitte Cuypers, Ann Kiyomura, Barry MacKay, Mike Machette, Charles Panui, Charlie Pasarell, Kristy Pigeon, Dennis Ralston, Judy Vincent, Val Ziegenfuss.
Los Angeles Strings:	John Alexander, Jean Baptiste Chanfreau, Pat Cramer, Kathy Harter, Geoff Masters, Marita Redondo, Karen Susman, Jerry Van Linge.
WTT FINALS *(in Denver & Philadelphia)*:	**(1W) Denver def. (1E) Philadelphia 55-45**

1975 TEAMS & PLAYERS:
EASTERN DIVISION

Boston Lobsters:	Bob Hewitt, Kerry Melville Reid, Raz Reid, Greer Stevens, Ion Tiriac, Wendy Turnbull, Valerie Ziegenfuss.
Cleveland Nets:	Bob Giltinan, Clark Graebner, Ann Hayden Jones, Marty Riessen, Sue Stap, Margo Tiff, Valerie Ziegenfuss.
Indiana Loves:	Roy Barth, Pat Bostrom, Carrie Meyer, Wendy Overton, Ray Ruffels, Allan Stone.
New York Sets:	Mona Guerrant, Billie Jean King, Sandy Mayer, Betsy Nagelsen, Charlie Owens, Fred Stolle, Virginia Wade.
Pittsburgh Triangles:	Mark Cox, Rayni Fox, Vitas Gerulaitis, Evonne Goolagong, Nancy Gunter, Peggy Michel, Kim Warwick.

WESTERN DIVISION

San Francisco Golden Gaters:	Dick Bohrnstedt, Ann Kiyomura, Ilana Kloss, Kate Latham, Frew McMillan, Tom Okker, Whitney Reed, Betty Stove. COACH: Frew McMillan
Hawaii Leis:	Mary Ann Beattie, Butch Buchholz, Joyce Champaigne, Margaret Court, Brigitte Cuypers, Heather Dahlgren, Owen Davidson, Tom Edlefsen, Helen Gourlay-Cawley, Kathy Kuykendall, John Newcombe, Barry MacKay, Charles Panui.
Los Angeles Strings:	Ross Case, Rosie Casals, Bob Lutz, Mike Machette, Geoff Masters, Bettyann Stuart.

Phoenix Racquets:	Jeff Austin, Pam Austin, Francoise Durr, Brian Fairlie, Andrew Pattison, Tony Roche, Kristien Kemmer-Shaw, Roger Taylor, Stephanie Tolleson.
San Diego Friars:	Ashok Amritraj, Vijay Amritraj, John Andrews, Jeff Cowan, Brigitte Cuypers, Helen Gourlay-Cawley, Lesley Hunt, Tom Leonard, Mike Machette, Dennis Ralston, Marita Redondo, Bill Schoen, Ken Stuart, Francis Troll, Janet Young.
WTT FINALS *(in Pittsburgh & San Francisco):*	(1E) Pittsburgh def. (1W) San Francisco 74-65 (25-26, 28-25 and 21-14)

1976 TEAMS & PLAYERS:
EASTERN DIVISION

Boston Lobsters:	John Alexander, Mike Estep, Kerry Melville Reid, Greer Stevens, Pam Teeguarden, Ion Tiriac
Cleveland Nets:	Raynie Fox, Bob Giltinan, Martina Navratilova, Wendy Overton, Haroon Rahim, Marty Riessen
Indiana Loves:	Syd Ball, Pat Bostrom, Mona Guerrant, Ann Kiyomura, Carrie Meyer, Ray Ruffels, Allan Stone
New York Sets:	Lindsey Beaven, Phil Dent, Billie Jean King, Sandy Mayer, Linda Siegelman, Fred Stolle, Virginia Wade. Coach: Fred Stolle
Pittsburgh Triangles:	Mark Cox, Evonne Goolagong, Vitas Gerulaitis, Peggy Michel, Bernie Mitton, Joanne Russell, Sue Stap

WESTERN DIVISION

San Francisco Golden Gaters:	Jeff Borowiak, Francoise Durr, Racquel Giscafre, John Lucas, Frew McMillan, Tom Okker, Betty Stove
Hawaii Leis:	Butch Buchholz, Margaret Court, Owen Davidson, Helen Gourlay-Cawley, Nancy Gunter, Marcie Louie, Ilie Nastase, Sue Stap
Los Angeles Strings:	Ashok Amritraj, Vijay Amritraj, Rosie Casals, Diane Fromholtz, Ann Haydon Jones, Bob Lutz, Charles Pasarell, Dennis Ralston
Phoenix Racquets:	Chris Evert, Andrew Pattison, Tony Roche, Kristien Kemmer-Shaw, Stephanie Tolleson, Butch Walts
San Diego Friars:	Ross Case, Cliff Drysdale, Terry Holladay, Rod Laver, Bettyann Stuart, Janet Young
WTT FINALS *(in New York & San Francisco):*	New York d. San Francisco 91-57 (31-23, 29-21, 31-13)

1977 TEAMS & PLAYERS:
EASTERN DIVISION

Boston Lobsters:	Roy Emerson, Mike Estep, Tony Roche, Virginia Ruzici, Greer Stevens, Martina Navratilova
Cleveland Nets:	Bjorn Borg, Bob Giltinan, Wendy Turnbull, Marty Riessen, Mariana Simionescu
Indiana Loves:	Syd Ball, Sue Barker, Ruta Gerulaitis, Vitas Gerulaitis, Ann Kiyomura, Allan Stone
New York Apples:	Lindsey Beaven, Billie Jean King, Sandy Mayer, Ray Ruffels, Linda Siegelman, Fred Stolle, Virginia Wade
The Soviets:	Natasha Chmyreva, Teimuraz Kakulia, Alex Metreveli, Olga Morozova

WESTERN DIVISION

Golden Gaters:	Francoise Durr, Frew McMillan, John Lucas, Tom Okker
Los Angeles Strings:	John Andrews, Rosie Casals, Dianne Fromholtz, Ilie Nastase, Charles Pasarell, Dennis Ralston
Phoenix Racquets:	Ross Case, Brian Cheney, Chris Evert, Kristien Shaw, Stephanie Tolleson, Butch Walts
San Diego Friars:	Julie Anthony, Cliff Drysdale, Mona Guerrant, Rod Laver, Kerry Melville Reid, Raz Reid
Sea-Port Cascades:	Pat Bostrom, Steve Docherty, Tom Gorman, Joanne Russell, Betty Stove, Erik van Dillen
WTT FINALS *(in New York & Phoenix):*	(2E) New York def. (1W) Phoenix 55-39

1978 TEAMS & PLAYERS:
EASTERN DIVISION:

Anaheim Oranges:	Anand Amritraj, Rosie Casals, Mark Cox, Cliff Drysdale, Francoise Durr, Kathy Harter. COACH: Cliff Drysdale
Boston Lobsters:	Roy Emerson, Mike Estep, Una Keyes, Martina Navratilova, Tony Roche, Greer Stevens, Anne Smith. COACH: Roy Emerson
Indiana Loves:	Diane Fromholtz, Tanya Harford, Sue Mappin, Geoff Masters, Allan Stone, John Whitlinger. COACH: Allan Stone
New York Apples:	Mary Carillo, Vitas Gerulaitis, Billie Jean King, Ray Ruffels, Joanne Russell, Fred Stolle. COACH: Fred Stolle
New Orleans Sun Belt Nets:	Helen Gourlay-Cawley, John Lucas, Andrew Pattison, Renee Richards, Marty Riessen, Wendy Turnbull. COACH: Marty Riessen

WESTERN DIVISION

Golden Gaters:	Ilana Kloss, Marise Kruger, Sandy Mayer, Frew McMillan, Virginia Wade, Michael Wayman. COACH: Frew McMillan

Los Angeles Strings:	Ashok Amritraj, Vijay Amritraj, Chris Evert, Ann Kiyomura, Ilie Nastase, Stephanie Tolleson. COACH: Ilie Nastase
Phoenix Racquets:	Syd Ball, Sue Barker, Raynie Fox, Dean Paul Martin, Jr., Kristien Kemmer-Shaw, Butch Walts.
San Diego Friars:	Ross Case, Mona Guerrant, Rod Laver, Kerry Reid Melville, Raz Reid, Janet Young. COACH: Rod Laver
Seattle Cascades:	Brigitte Cuypers, Tom Gorman, Chris Kachel, Marita Redondo, Sherwood Stewart, Betty Stove. COACH: Tom Gorman
WTT FINALS *(in Los Angeles / Boston):*	(2W) Los Angeles def. (1E) Boston 108-93

World TeamTennis started on May 6, 1974, in a huge spectacle at Philadelphia's massive sports arena, the Spectrum, as the Philadelphia Freedoms initiated the league into action against the Pittsburgh Triangles. That match would set off the league, which was the first professional sports league to be created since the National Basketball Association came into fruition on November 1, 1946. So, nearly 30 years later, the United States finally had a new professional sports league to rally behind.

At the Spectrum, they certainly got a show. Although a storm dampened the weather for the match, it was filled with over 10,000 spectators, according to *The Art of World TeamTennis*, a book detailing the league's first years.

***

Billie Jean King, who had been drafted first and selected by the Philadelphia Freedoms, found herself in action that night against Evonne Goolagong of the Pittsburgh Triangles.

A replica of the Liberty Bell was wheeled onto the court during the opening ceremony, and the crowd proved electric: a first, no doubt, for a tennis match. After all, the league promoted audience participation back then, including cheering for their teams as play wore on and allowing for fans to be boisterous and expressive. Compare that to Wimbledon, the most prestigious of tennis events, where players at the All England Club must dress pristinely and in all white. Noise, meanwhile, is highly discouraged, even after points, in order to honor tradition.

But it couldn't have been more different for WTT's debut. And the historic match on May 6 was won by King and her Freedoms squad 31 to 25. With that match, another history for sports was made, too—the first fully integrated men's and women's sports teams were competing against one another in a league in which equality served at the forefront.

The Philadelphia Freedoms finished second in 1974, which was the league's inaugural season. Pictured (l. to r.): Player/coach Billie Jean King, Fred Stolle, Brian Fairlie, Julie Anthony, Buster Mottram and Kathy Kuykendall. Photo: World TeamTennis

For instance, King was the coach for the Freedoms that year, working with the likes of Fred Stolle, Julie Anthony, Brian Fairlie, Tory-Ann Fretz, Kathy Kuykendall, and Buster Mottram. Dick Butera, a real estate developer, owned the Freedoms.

"It was totally exciting having ten thousand people watching a match in the Spectrum," said Larry King about the match.

"We responded to the crowd in a positive manner," said Billie Jean King after the match. "Tennis has finally begun relating to the masses, and people are really going to start getting turned on to the sport. It may take five years, but it's gonna happen."

"We took the tennis to the people," said King in a 2016 interview.

***

A couple of quirky things of note happened those first seasons, making WTT a standout professional sport and one for the history books. But in this very special case, it was one for the song books.

Acclaimed singer and songwriter Sir Elton John of the United Kingdom and Billie Jean King became fast friends after meeting in the 1970s. During the summer of 1974, John recorded what's now one of his most well-known songs in honor of King's WTT team. The song, dubbed "Philadelphia Freedom," was one he recorded during breaks between sessions for *Captain Fantastic and the Brown Dirt Cowboy*.

Although "Philadelphia Freedom" wasn't released officially until 1975, the song became one of his most popular hits in the U.S., climbing to the top spot. The song would end up symbolizing just the start of a powerful friendship between the two legends in their respective fields. Moreover, it would kick off a series of events in the United States, called "Smash Hits" (which was the brain child of Ilana Kloss), jointly held by John and King, which would go on to raise millions for AIDs research.

***

In an interview with Elton John's web site, King discussed the importance of the song and the first time she met the music legend.

"Philadelphia Freedom" wouldn't be available for purchase until *Elton John's Greatest Hits Volume 2* in 1977. The standalone single was his second after "Lucy in the Sky with Diamonds," according to his web site. It entered the Billboard charts at number 53 on March 8 of that year.

"Five weeks later it reached the #1 position, where it stayed for two weeks, and spent a total of five months on the chart overall," according to a history of the song. "Written on the label of the vinyl 45 RPM single were the words, 'with Love to B.J.K. and the sound of Philadelphia.'"

But the history of "Philadelphia Freedom" goes back to over a year before it was ever recorded. That's when King met John in September 1973. At the time, Elton was in the United States on a sold-out tour to release *Goodbye Yellow Brick Road*, which would be one of his most successful albums in a star-studded and illustrious career.

Billie Jean King, already one of the greatest female tennis players of all time ahead of meeting Elton John, had just won her fifth Wimbledon title. She was just about to take on Bobby Riggs in the "Battle of the Sexes" match, which would change not only tennis but also the way in which gender equality was talked about in the U.S. and abroad.

In an interview years after the song climbed to the top of the Billboard chart, King spoke about meeting John. "[Promoter] Jerry Perenchio threw a party two weeks before the King/Riggs match in September of '73 in Los Angeles," she explained. "When I got to the party I said, 'Jerry, it's great to see you…what's this party for? Is it for you?' And he said, 'Oh no, it's for Elton John.' I said, 'Elton John? He's my favorite! Are you kidding?'"

King reminisced that the chance to meet a music celebrity "brought back memories of when I first heard 'Your Song' in 1971, I think. I was driving the hills of San Francisco, on Van Ness Street. I remember having to pull over to listen to it. I love anything with anybody playing keyboards. And of course on top of that he can sing unbelievably well. So I fell in love with Elton and 'Your Song' and I had all his albums up to that time."

"So we're at the party. Elton's across the room from me. He keeps looking at me… I keep looking at him. And finally Tony King, who actually is still with him, comes over and says, 'This is ridiculous. Elton's been dying to meet you all night but he's too shy,'" she said in the interview. "And I remember I looked at Tony and said, 'Ditto.'" That served as the perfect timing for the two to meet one another.

"So Tony says, 'Come with me…' and I get up and he sits me across from Elton and says, 'Elton this is Billie. Billie this is Elton. Okay…now…talk!'" she said. King recalled that the two "hit it off." He asked her when she'd next be in England and Wimbledon was coming up. Although she never thought the two would see each other again, nine months later, she arrived at London's Gloucester Hotel and had a note from him waiting.

"I don't know how the heck he found out where I'd be staying. The note said, 'Please call me.' And I almost didn't call," she said. "I was too shy."

Elton John wrote his hit song 'Philadelphia Freedom' for close friend Billie Jean King and her signature WTT franchise, the Philadelphia Freedoms. John was often at WTT matches, sitting on the bench with the Freedoms. Photo: Terry O'Neill

Vitas Gerulaitis playing during the early days of World TeamTennis. Photo: CameraworkUSA

But King mustered the courage to call him, and he picked her up in his Rolls Royce with 28 speakers. "'What should we do?' I said, 'I don't care. Whatever you want.' He said, "Well, I don't wanna be in the hotel, let's just sit in the car and talk.'" They ended up talking for hours.

King recalled the first time they discussed him writing a song for her. "In the summer of 1974 we were driving to one of his concerts, and he looked over at me in the back of the car (I can remember, he was on my right), and he said, 'I want to write a song for you.'"

But she was incredulous. "I turned scarlet red, I'm sure, and went, 'Oh please. What?' And he goes, 'No, I want to write a song, what are we gonna call it?' And I said [exasperatedly], 'I don't know!' Then he went, 'How about "Philadelphia Freedom"?' Because I played for the [World TeamTennis] Philadelphia Freedoms, and he used to come watch our matches."

That, of course, would end up being just what the hit song was to be called.

***

King recalls getting John a uniform made by the Freedoms' designer Ted Tingling. "I had Elton fitted at a hotel in Philadelphia, and he would come to the matches and sit on the bench in his uniform, and he'd just go nuts and scream at me to do better," she said in the interview. "It was hysterical! It was great. He was really intense…so enthusiastic."

She said she was thrilled by the choice to name the song "Philadelphia Freedom." "I said, 'That's great. It will be a great gift to the people of Philadelphia.'" With the song released officially a year after for the Bicentennial, King said that its timing was perfect, too.

"And I love the word 'freedom.' I would say it is one of my all-time favorite words since I was a child. I remember talking about freedom in elementary school," she said. "And I am the one who named the team the Philadelphia Freedoms. And then in 2009 I got the Medal of Freedom from President Obama," added King. "It just goes on and on."

She first heard the song during the playoff game in the first season of the league. It was August 25, 1974, and he asked if she wanted to hear the rough mix. He was nervous, she said, and she tried to comfort him. "'Do you mind if I have the team listen with me?'" she continued. "And we're in the locker room…not real spiffy…and he put it the cassette player on the trainer's table, and I loved it within the first three notes."

She continued: "I said, 'I don't like it, Elton, I love it, love it, love it.' He said, 'We don't have to understand what the words mean…' and I said, 'It doesn't matter. It's the emotion of it.'" King doesn't mind it isn't about tennis either, especially since it's celebrated as an anthem to the people of Philadelphia.

Larry King recalls when "Philadelphia Freedom" was played for the first time, too. "But you know what was funny? They were in the playoffs that first season, then Elton John came to a game against the Denver Racquets, and he had the first rough mix of Philadelphia Freedom," he said, "and he played it in the locker room and the Denver Coliseum. That was the first time we heard Philadelphia Freedom."

***

While the Freedoms won that first match against Pittsburgh that night, it was just the first of many matches played on WTT's courts. In the first year, 16 squads signed up to play WTT with teams in Baltimore, Boston, Buffalo-Toronto, Chicago, Cleveland, Denver, Detroit, Florida (Miami), Hawaii (Honolulu), Houston, Los Angeles, Minnesota (Minneapolis-St.Paul), New York, Philadelphia, Pittsburgh, and San Francisco.

And while the Freedoms, led by King, finished in the Atlantic Section of the league's Eastern Division with 39 wins to just five losses and with the league MVP recognition going to King, they faced a tough test in the Denver Racquets for that first season in the championship round.

To get to that stage of the historic first season, the Freedoms advanced to the Eastern Division Championship Series to face the Pittsburgh Triangles. There the Freedoms played a series against Pittsburgh in a rematch of the first ever WTT match. The Freedoms won the series against their rival team by 52-45 overall, sending them to the league's first finals.

In the championship match, on August 25, King lost the opening set to Francois Durr, "setting the tone for the Freedoms' uphill struggle," according to *The Art of World TeamTennis*. "Philadelphia had lost each of the first four sets."

The account continued: "The Racquets' Andrew Pattison knocked off Brian Fairlie in men's singles, Durr and Kristien Kemmer [Shaw] defeated Julie Anthony and Billie Jean in women's doubles. Denver's men's doubles victory mathematically clinched the win for the Racquets because it put them ahead by ten games, 25-15."

But the Freedoms didn't go down without a fight heading into the final set, which was mixed doubles. Indeed, Anthony and Stolle rallied to secure a 6-2 win over Kemmer and Roche, ensuring that the top team during the regular season wasn't handed a shutout ahead of the final match of the season the next evening in Philadelphia's Spectrum.

"They were all over us," said King after the match to the press. "There was no way we could concentrate," she added. In an interview, King said that she made one of the worst coaching decisions ever by making the call to have her team play their first match away instead of in Philadelphia.

The next night, the momentum nabbed by the Freedoms in the mixed doubles set, which sparked a glimmer of hope in a more competitive match, continued a little. King took to the court at the Spectrum, which had thousands in attendance, to grab a 4-0 lead. But Durr, her opponent, fought back. While King won 6-4 ultimately to close out women's singles, the men's singles match went in Denver's favor when Andrew Pattison won 6-0.

With women's doubles and men's doubles following, the score was nearly equal at 22-20 in favor of Denver.

The first championship came down to mixed doubles. Kristien Kemmer and Tony Roche clinched the match and the first WTT final with a 6-4 win over Anthony and Stolle to close out the season and claim the Teflon Cup.

Billie Jean King and Fred Stolle, here in 1975 with the New York sets, competed on the same team teams numerous times during the 1970s. Photo: World TeamTennis

***

To make that first season a possibility, months and months of planning and preparation took place with an idea originally born out of a risky plan by a group who wanted to take the tennis world by storm with an innovative concept. Larry King and Billie Jean King, meanwhile, would go on to spearhead that effort and ultimately make it a household name during the '70s and beyond.

Of course, as background, the fledgling women's tennis association was still only years old thanks to the work of Billie Jean King, Gladys Heldman (the editor of *World Tennis Magazine*), and the "Original 9," including King, Rosie Casals, Nancy Gunter, Peaches Bartkowicz, Valerie Ziegenfuss, Kristy Pigeon, Judy Dalton, Kerry Melville, and Julie Heldman. These women fought hard against the tennis establishment, including the United States Tennis Lawn Association (USTLA), which attempted to bar women from competing in tennis for money.

But the Original 9 would not be stopped, despite players being threatened to be suspended from USLTA and ILTF-sanctioned events. Their actions, however, would allow women to have the option to compete professionally in similar fashion to the men.

"I get all the kudos, but the eight players here did just as much or sometimes more," King said in an interview with ESPN about the efforts to begin a women's tour.

"We had no idea that this little dollar would turn into millions," Casals added.

Indeed, with the nine women athletes and Heldman, the fight for women's tennis proved successful. But the backbone for that support came from King's husband, Larry King, an attorney, who helped drum up the support needed to put their efforts into action. King tirelessly lobbied during those early days with tournament directors and with other businessmen in the industry to make professional tournaments for the women a reality.

At the same time, opportunities started blossoming for women athletes, especially through the passage of Title IX in 1972, giving women attending college the ability to compete for scholarship money for the first time. With this and the women's liberation movement gaining steam from the late '60s and early '70s, which saw women demanding ideals of equality both at work and at home, the groundwork was being laid for something like a professional sports league treating men and women fairly. Of course, this was easier said than done.

***

Billie Jean King has been a champion for equal rights throughout her legendary career. Photo: CameraworkUSA

1971 proved to be a turning point for the efforts of the Kings, the Original 9, and Gladys Heldman, although not without complications. In January of that year and with Heldman at the head of the newly created women's circuit through the sponsorship of Virginia Slims, the first tournament was played. By 1973, the circuit would become the Women's Tennis Association, as it's known today and which Billie Jean King founded.

As the year wore on, women's events run by Virginia Slims and the Women's Pro Tour Circuit (as it was dubbed) offered no less than $20,000 per event and without USLTA sanction. But of course it didn't go as smoothly as desired by the players fighting to make ends meet as pro female athletes. The pressure ultimately got to Heldman, who said that she wanted to step down from her position in 1972.

According to *The Art of World TeamTennis*, the fact that Heldman wanted to leave her post atop the women's game prompted a chain reaction of events that would lead to the formation of WTT: "The unexpected announcement prompted Shari Barman, a Virginia Slims circuit player, to write her father, expressing doubts about the future of the tour. She solicited his help. Though Shari didn't know it at the time, her letter of August 20, 1972, was the seed of conception that resulted in the birth of World TeamTennis."

Her letter underscored the grave reality of a fledgling women's tour. Despite being monumental in creating the professional league for women to play tennis, the effort was ripe with complications in its relationships to the other circuits.

Her letter underscored her own fear of the unknown for the sport of women's tennis and proved indicative of what her colleagues probably felt as well. Here's what that fateful message, which was written from Newport, detailed to her father, a Beverly Hills business manager with a slate of top-notch clients, including actors and pro athletes:

Dear Dad:

The circuit this summer is *very* bad—disorganized and it looks as though if something doesn't happen soon to get it together there will be no more Virginia Slims circuit—We need a new promoter and manager now that Gladys Heldman is no longer with the group… Anyway, we are in quite a predicament…Do you have any ideas on the subject? I've been talking to Billie Jean a lot and I told her I was going to talk to you about it.

Well, that's all for now—will be talking to you soon.

Love from Shari

And with that Barman mobilized her father into action. Understandably, he didn't want his daughter in distress over the future of her career and the careers of other female professional athletes.

As *The Art of World TeamTennis* states, Barman called Dennis Murphy, who at the time was the general manager of the World Hockey Association's Los Angeles Sharks, a client with whom Barman worked at the time.

Together, they approached Larry King, along with Gary Davidson, who had founded the American Basketball Association with Murphy. They went to King to ask him for advice about the fate of women's tennis and to take control of the circuit from Heldman after her departure. But he was adamant that she wouldn't leave, but rather would attempt to start a new circuit for the benefit of women athletes, according to the book.

That discussion, however, prompted the inkling of a new idea based on circumstances of the women's circuit at the time: there was no play being held during the summer months between Wimbledon and Forest Hills (or the US Open as it's known today) in Queens, New York. The fact that there were months open for potential tennis events in the country and not in Europe (which some had played and were tired of all the traveling), signaled an opportunity.

The idea of a summer circuit was floated to King, who didn't want to join them as a partner, but rather wanted to be hired to help run it. On September 20, 1972, the three men met in Oakland, California, to discuss the summer circuit in a discussion that continued into the new year.

They talked about a separate league that was selling franchises and decided that they, too, wanted to create a league, as opposed to a summer circuit. King became excited by the opportunity and said he'd become a partner in such an organization. Murphy suggested that Jordan Kaiser, a World Hockey Association friend, should come on board to manage finances.

A month later on February 5, 1973, according to *The Art of World TeamTennis*, the four men met at the Palm Springs Racquet Club. With Kaiser on board as a partner, along with Murphy and King, Barman became the director.

Together they started the International Professional Tennis League, or IPTL.

With the idea for a new league underway, the men decided that they wanted to have twelve franchises for the first season, which was to start the following April. They wanted to enlist star power to play in the league, including, of course, Billie Jean King and Rod Laver.

But the National Tennis League, which had been looking to sell franchises and which inspired the IPTL into action, got wind of the rival's formation. They apparently threatened to sue the new league for infringement on the idea.

However, the two groups would never get to court. Instead, they settled and merged, with the men from Pittsburgh from the NTL offered a franchise in the city to get on board.

That, therefore, is how World TeamTennis got its name. With the merger, the name was changed to what it is to this day.

Over the next months, the four founders of WTT worked to get the league into shape for a 1974 first season. That meant they needed to fend off challenges from other organizations like the Association of Tennis Professionals for the men, hammer down the schedule and number of franchises for the league, as well as put into place a system to ensure it would run smoothly.

To do so, the founding fathers prepared a variety of essentials for the league's success, including operation, budget, and losses expected, and they set up a meeting for later that year on May 22 for those interested in pursuing franchises in Chicago. Again, the first season was expected to begin in May of 1974, and time was ticking.

***

Highlight #1: Larry King: The WTT Mastermind

League co-founders Larry King and Billie Jean King (pictured with their dog Lucy) were tireless in their promotion of World TeamTennis throughout the league's early years in the 1970s. Photo: World TeamTennis

Larry King, the husband to Billie Jean King at the time the league kicked off, proved to be one of the greatest visionaries for the promotion of tennis. King, a California native, helped lead the creation of the women's tennis association as an attorney and tennis promoter over the years.

King was born in Dayton, Ohio, in 1945 and married Billie Jean 20 years later. Their union would change tennis forever, given their ability to think ahead and promote equality in the sport. Indeed, their brainstorming and passion for teamwork led to the creation of World TeamTennis, a league that would never have come to fruition or continuity without King's tireless efforts.

That belief in WTT as the future of the sport was something he brought with him from the very beginning when he was first asked to help lead the league's formation.

"Having a team sport for tennis, that one I'd be willing to be on," King recalled, "because I believe that's the future in this country."

But given the promotion of equality on the court, with men and women playing together, there was some backlash, King explained.

"Because of the men and women aspect, it was a real social revolution to have teams that [had] together males and females," he said, "and it was really socially such a much better deal for the athletes."

The idea of men and women having the opportunity to interact and hit with one another was a boon for both genders, though. "It gave you practice partners, and it gave you practice partners for the tour," said King.

"Probably the most amazing statistic is that you look at that first Wimbledon where World TeamTennis players played, and World TeamTennis players have played May and June before Wimbledon, and you look at who made the quarters at the Wimbledon tournament in June," he added, "and seven out of the eight were TeamTennis players."

Said King, "If you wanted to know whether team tennis was good for the sport or not, just look at the results."

And as King took the reins of the league early on in its creation as a result of a lack of leadership, he also helped revive the league in the early '80s after it went on a hiatus.

But during his times, there's one anecdote that sticks out about his commitment to growing the team concept. In 1976 and 1977, a team from the Soviet Union took part in the WTT concept.

But it only came to fruition thanks to King's diplomacy.

"I went to the Soviet Union and made a deal with the Soviets that we play three exhibitions in Russia and they would send a team to play the summer, and we called them the Keystones, but they only played occasionally in Pennsylvania," said King of the traveling team for WTT.

He continued, "Everything back at the Soviet Union was done person to person. They had to look one in the face and say whether they trust you or not."

King had been talking to the Russians beginning the year before at the US Open, which prompted the idea to have a Soviet team on board. He gave them a proposal, but they didn't sign it.

King, however, was getting antsy about a response.

"I didn't hear anything until Christmas, and they never responded to my proposal. They just said, 'Okay, well, come to Moscow and we'll make a deal.' They ran us around to meet all these people, and we're getting down to the end and I said, 'I'm leaving this. What's the deal?'"

Their response: "'Your proposal, we translated it into Russian and we'll sign your deal,'" said King. "That was it."

***

And so the two-day meeting arrived as the preparations for a first season of World TeamTennis began in earnest. The league elected George McCall, who was fielding a job application to be hired with the ATP. He turned down the job offer and became the first commissioner of the league.

Fourteen interested and potential franchise owners also arrived at the meetings despite concerns that the meeting would come and go without any interested parties. Those fourteen franchise owners plus the Pittsburgh franchise that was organized after the merger with the NTL meant a potential for 15 teams for the first season.

But a league with an odd number of teams would be, understandably, difficult to pull off. And instead of cutting down the number of teams vying to play in the inaugural season, Gary Davidson, an American

Basketball Association co-founder, ended up purchasing a franchise to get the total to 16—just the right number for a league.

"In an amazingly brief period, a revolutionary sports league had been conceived, a completely unique format had been devised, a potentially disastrous lawsuit had been circumvented, an organized counter-move had been thwarted, a commissioner had been hired and, perhaps most important," according to *The Art of World TeamTennis,* "sixteen franchises had been sold."

***

But with the franchises found, there was still much more work to be done in a short amount of time. With the franchise owners found and teams sold, WTT still proved to be missing one key ingredient for success: players. To be more specific, 96 of them, since each team needed to field six players total, including three men and three women.

With an official player draft scheduled for August of 1973, owners decided to try to snag the world's top players ahead of time to stack their teams. Although there was uncertainty initially surrounding who would ultimately sign on to play that first season, huge players like Billie Jean King and John Newcombe agreed to sign on.

The draft took place on August 3, with Florida getting the first draft selection. The franchise, unsurprisingly, chose Chris Evert, while a young Bjorn Borg was also selected in the first round by the Cleveland Nets. Notably, Evert wouldn't play until 1976 when she played for the Phoenix Racquets (she'd play again for the team in 1977 as well as in 1978 for the championship-winning Los Angeles Strings).

The New York Apples celebrate the 1977 WTT championship. Pictured (l. to r.): Virginia Wade, Fred Stolle, team owner Sol Berg, Sandy Mayer, Billie Jean King and Lindsay Beaven. Photo: World TeamTennis

Overall, 310 players were chosen by the sixteen franchises over the course of 20 rounds. Other players who were drafted included Stan Smith, Arthur Ashe and Bobby Riggs, famous for playing against Billie Jean King in the Battle of the Sexes in September a month later.

As the year wore on and regulations by tennis other governing bodies, such as the ATP, began to loosen, players began signing up for WTT franchises. No longer were they afraid that they'd be suspended for playing in the new, team-oriented league. The USLTA, the ILTF, and the WCT all joined in to take neutral positions regarding the league, which paved the way for the first season to begin a few short months later.

Each player would play forty-four matches during the season with one of the franchises, which were split up by divisions as well as sections. "World TeamTennis had confronted the powerful tennis establishment and, despite overwhelming odds, had won the right to exist," according to *The Art of World TeamTennis*. "A little luck and a lot of hard work had brought WTT to the threshold of its first season."

WTT FINALS 1974

Denver Racquets 55

(27-21, 28-24) *

Philadelphia Freedoms 48

* From 1974-1978, championship matches were either best 2 out of 3 matches or 3 out of 5 matches.

WTT FINALS 1975

Pittsburgh Triangles 74

(25-26, 28-25, 21-14) *

San Francisco Golden Gaters 65

* From 1974-1978, championship matches were either best 2 out of 3 matches or 3 out of 5 matches.

WTT FINALS 1976

New York Sets 91

(31-23, 29-21, 31-13) *

San Francisco Golden Gaters 57

* From 1974-1978, championship matches were either best 2 out of 3 matches or 3 out of 5 matches.

WTT FINALS **1977**

New York Apples

(27-22, 28-17) *

Phoenix Racquets

*From 1974-1978, championship matches were either best
2 out of 3 matches or 3 out of 5 matches.*

WTT FINALS **1978**

Los Angeles Strings

(24-21, 30-20, 26-27, 28-25) *

Boston Lobsters

*From 1974-1978, championship matches were either best
2 out of 3 matches or 3 out of 5 matches.*

Chapter Two: Seasons Six to Ten (1981-1985):

The League Rebuilds

1981 TEAMS & PLAYERS:

California Oranges:	Anand Amritraj, Barbara Potter, Marty Riessen, Sherwood Stewart, Sharon Walsh.
Los Angeles Strings:	Vijay Amritraj, Terry Holladay, Martina Navratilova, Trey Waltke.
Oakland Breakers:	John Austin, Fritz Buehning, Phil Dent, Billie Jean King, Ann Kiyomura, Ilana Kloss, Bernie Mitton, Peter Rennert.
San Diego Friars:	Leslie Allen, Ross Case, Mary Lou Piatek-Daniels, Butch Walts.
WTT FINALS:	Los Angeles Strings (determined by best regular season record)

1982 TEAMS & PLAYERS:

California Oranges:	Sandy Collins, Terry Moor, Stacy Margolin, Brian Teacher, Vincent Van Patten. COACH: Virginia Brown
Chicago Aces:	Laura Dupont, Tim Gullickson, Steve Krulevitz, Betsy Nagelsen. COACH: Rick Vetter
Dallas Stars:	Kevin Curren, Steven Denton, Zina Garrison-Jackson, Joanne Russell, Anne Smith, Sharon Walsh-Pete. COACH: Warren Jacques
Houston Astro-Knots:	John Austin, Rosalyn Fairbank, Bruce Nichols, Wendy White. COACH: Owen Davidson
Los Angeles Strings:	Vijay Amritraj, Billie Jean King, Trey Waltke, Ilana Kloss. COACH: Vijay Amritraj
Oakland Breakers:	Leslie Allen, Rosie Casals, Bob Hewitt, Peter Rennert. COACH: Bob Hewitt
Phoenix Sunsets:	Tom Gullickson, Ann Kiyomura, Andy Pattison, Pam Teeguarden. COACH: Andy Pattison
San Diego Friars:	Ross Case, Mary Lou Piatek-Daniels, Candy Reynolds, Butch Walts. COACH: Larry Willens
WTT FINALS (in Phoenix, Ariz.):	Dallas Stars def. Phoenix Sunsets 27-22

1983 TEAMS & PLAYERS:

Arizona Racquets:	Pat Dupre, Ann Kiyomura, Andy Pattison, Pam Teeguarden. COACH: Andy Pattison
California Oranges:	John Austin, Sandy Collins, Mima Jausovec, Robert Van't Hof. COACH: Virginia Brown
Chicago Fyre:	Lloyd Bourne, Billie Jean King, Sharon Walsh, Trey Waltke. COACH: Ilana Kloss
Dallas Stars:	Mike Estep, Dick Stockton, Wendy White. COACH: Dick Stockton
Houston Astro-Knots:	Tony Giammalva, Yvonne Vermaak, Kim Warwick, Nancy Yeargin.
Indiana Loves:	Syd Ball, Stacy Margolin, Kim Schaefer. COACH: Syd Ball
Los Angeles Strings:	Barbara Hallquist, Chip Hooper, Larry Stefanki, Anne White.
San Diego Friars:	Rosie Casals, Ross Case, Mary Lou Piatek-Daniels, Butch Walts. COACH: Rosie Casals
WTT FINALS (in Los Angeles, Calif).:	Chicago Fyre def. Los Angeles Strings 26-20

1984 TEAMS & PLAYERS:

Boston Bays:	Owen Davidson, Beth Herr, Ann Kiyomura, Bill Scanlon
Chicago Fyre:	Billie Jean King, Ben Testerman, Sharon Walsh-Pete, Trey Waltke
Long Beach Breakers:	Ilana Kloss, Larry Stefanki, Robert Van't Hof, Anne White. COACH: Lorne Kuhle
Los Angeles Strings:	Lisa Bonder, Terry Holladay, Sherwood Stewart, Roscoe Tanner
San Diego Buds:	Ross Case, Brad Gilbert, Andrea Leand, Pam Teeguarden
St. Louis Eagles:	Rosie Casals, Drew Gitlin, Kim Schaefer, Vince Van Patten
WTT FINALS (in Los Angeles, Calif.):	*San Diego Buds d. Long Beach Breakers 30-13

*season consisted of one-week tournament

1985 TEAMS & PLAYERS:

Boston Bays:	Drew Gitlin, Ann Henricksson, Mike Leach, Andrea Leand. COACH: Owen Davidson
Chicago Fire:	Rosie Casals, Terry Holladay, Nduka Odizor, Ben Testerman. COACH: Ilana Kloss
Los Angeles Strings:	Larry Stefanki, Pam Teeguarden, Anne White, Vince Van Patten. COACH: Lornie Kuhle
Miami Beach Breakers:	Ilana Kloss, Steve Meister, Yvonne Vermaak, Van Winitsky. COACH: Ilana Kloss
Oakland Aces:	Marty Davis, Chris Dunk, Barbara Jordan, Sharon Walsh Pete. COACH: Lynne Rolley

San Antonio Racquets:	Tony Giammalva, Hank Pfister, Kim Schaefer, Anne Smith. COACH: Clarence Mabry
San Diego Buds:	Todd Nelson, Mary Lou Piatek-Daniels, Butch Walts, Robin White. COACH: Larry Willens
St. Louis Slims:	Sandy Collins, John Mattke, Terry Moor, Candy Reynolds. COACH: Virginia Brown
WTT FINALS *(in San Antonio, Texas):*	San Diego Buds def. St. Louis Slims 25-24

After the first five seasons came to a close in 1978, the league stopped operating for a couple years until 1981. There were a number of reasons that led to the decision to end operations, with personnel issues at the forefront, according to Larry King and research from the league's archives.

A number of teams disbanded, one after the other, once the 1978 season came to an end. The commissioner at the time, Butch Buchholz, stepped down from the league during that period as well.

In addition, between October and November following the season's end, the New York Apples, the Boston Lobsters, the Los Angeles Strings, the San Diego Friars, and the Indiana Loves announced that they would be disbanding. As a result, there were just five teams, down from 10 total.

But more teams would stop, too, with the Nets, the Anaheims, and the Seattle Cascades also announcing that they were shuttering operations. That unfortunately left just two teams; certainly not enough to continue a league that had been otherwise off to a fine start in its first seasons of play.

***

While WTT ended for a couple years, it wasn't for long. Indeed, the league began anew in 1981 with a renewed purpose to grow once again thanks to the guidance and spirited determination of Larry King, the co-founder of the league's first phase and a champion for equality in tennis, with Billie Jean King by his side.

Once the league resumed play, it was with a completely different format than before. As opposed to the 16 franchises spread out across the United States, WTT began its first season back with just four, California-based teams.

The franchises that took part in the relaunch were the Oakland Breakers, the Los Angeles Strings, the San Diego Friars, and the California Oranges.

"That it is often difficult, and sometimes downright impossible to keep a good idea down is a little slice of reality that was nicely illustrated by a certain event that occurred recently," began a write-up in the 1981 *Supertiebreaker* media guide released by the league in honor of the season.

"The date was March 24, 1981; the place was the press lounge of the Forum in Los Angeles," it continued, "and the event in question was a press conference at which it was announced that TeamTennis had been born again."

Larry King announced the revival of the league, the passage continues. After all, King became the president of the new league. But his announcement fell on mostly deaf ears when he spoke to the media gathered together. At least, that's according to the article.

"Although King took great pains to stress the fact that TeamTennis was a brand new venture and not merely World TeamTennis, Part II; several of the assembled media types failed to make the distinction right away," it read. "In fact, the first question fired at King went a little something like this: 'Why are you starting team tennis again when everyone knows that World TeamTennis was a dismal failure?'"

Harsh words and a not-so-warm welcome for the league's new beginning. But King was prepared for getting such a hostile question.

He responded with poise. "What most people don't realize is that WTT didn't collapse because of financial difficulties," he began. "Obviously, the owners lost a lot of money during the early going, but the league was actually prospering at the box office when it folded."

King said that there was actually another issue that caused the league to end. "No, it wasn't money problems that killed WTT, it was a number of serious organizational difficulties that did it," he clarified, including how owners were fighting internally.

But the media wasn't sold on the explanation. One asked exactly how the new league would ensure that the same issues were prevented in the future. "Simple," responded King. "The TeamTennis organization is centralized at the league level. Because the league is solely responsible for acquiring and paying the players, the individual team owners and operators are free to concentrate their efforts on promoting and staging TeamTennis matches in their respective markets."

And while the organizational issues proved to be a reason for the league's demise the first time around, the passion of the players and WTT executives to bring it back was even greater.

"The truth was that King and a small, hard-core cadre of team tennis people were unwilling to accept the demise of WTT," said the article. "They could deal with the collapse because the league was merely a vehicle for the concept of TeamTennis, but they weren't about to let the concept die. No way."

***

Obstacles, of course, existed as the league looked to reestablish itself. But thankfully King and the others working on WTT learned from the mistakes of the past to pursue the development of an even stronger league for the future.

But to do that, King decided the league needed to offer a different experience to fans as well as a unique approach in other ways. "As the structure of TeamTennis began to take shape, it was apparent the new league's basic philosophy was approximately 180 degrees away from that of its predecessor," according to a *Supertiebreaker* from the period.

"Where WTT had swept flamboyantly into the tennis arena like a plaid-jacketed, overly-boisterous guest arriving at a quiet, black-tie dinner party, TeamTennis would make a more sedate dignified entrance."

Roy Emerson played three seasons of World TeamTennis during the 1970s. Photo: World TeamTennis

For instance, the new league wouldn't focus so much on the amount of money players were making for their commitment to playing during the season. Moreover, the league decided to stay humble in its announcements. "Nor would there be any proud proclamations that TeamTennis would start with 48 teams and expand from there," according to the article.

To that effect, the four teams involved in the revival of WTT would play a vastly different schedule than in the previous five seasons before the hiatus. Instead of dozens of matches, on March 24 the league announced that the teams would each play 12 matches over a three-week season.

That first season there were 50 applications for 16 total roster positions in the league with Billie Jean King, Martina Navratilova, Terry Holladay, Vijay Amritraj and Marty Riessen signing up to play.

A large part of the team's revival came due to a new innovation with a pivotal part of the league and concerned the athletes playing during the new, three-week season.

"But there was something else to be tested as well," according to a *Supertiebreaker* article from 1982, "something nearly as vital to the success of TeamTennis as putting bodies in the seats: the league's unique method of compensating its players."

It continued, "Actually, it wasn't the compensation plan that was unique, just its application to a professional sports league." Meaning: players weren't given the same sort of individual salaries trumpeted to the media as in the previous seasons.

Instead, the way players earned their money for the season followed in the steps of a typical tournament's; it became performance based. "In still other words, the TeamTennis season would essentially be a three-week tournament with a purse of $305,000."

The winning team for that first season? The Los Angeles Strings, which was based on their performance over the three weeks. They ended up winning the season with a record of nine wins to just three losses.

Martina Navratilova played for the Los Angeles Strings in 1981 during her historic WTT career. Pictured (l. to r.): Trey Waltke, Vijay Amritraj, Martina Navratilova and Terry Holladay. Photo: World TeamTennis

They wouldn't ultimately appear poised for victory right out of the gate. In fact, the team lost three of their first four matches to begin it, before rattling off eight straight wins to beat out their competition. However, they turned their form around. Martina Navratilova helped secure the Strings' victory that year by being a dominant force in women's singles. She came out first in women's doubles and mixed doubles as well.

"But last summer's real bottom line was that TeamTennis had come through the experiment with flying colors," according to the *Supertiebreaker*. "The team was exciting and entertaining, the fans showed up at the turnstiles, and the compensation plan worked like a charm while nicely illustrating that each TeamTennis point is extremely important.

***

Season two brought substantial growth to the league after a massive expansion from the first year back after the hiatus. In fact, the league doubled in size to eight teams and partnered with Nike to help make it happen.

As part of the expanded number of teams, each played more matches throughout the three-week season: 14 versus 12 in 1981. And the clear favorites throughout the season were the Dallas Stars, who dominated the regular season by claiming a 12-2 record.

Billie Jean King spoke with praise about the league's format upon its revival, especially with the opportunity to face Martina Navratilova, one of her main rivals during Women's Tennis Association matches, so frequently that summer.

"We played in half the matches," King recalled of the 1981 season when she played for the Oakland Breakers, which included a different format from previous years. "It was like having Kareem Abdul-Jabbar and Larry Bird play in every other NBA game."

From the very beginning, they proved to be a powerful team with a strong playing dynamic. The team was comprised of Anne Smith, Sharon Walsh, Kevin Curren, and Steve Denton. Together they took out the Houston Astro-Knots in a 30-8 demolition.

Other teams that proved to be no match for the Stars that season? Chicago, California, Phoenix, and San Diego even though the team lost their No. 1 women's player, Smith, to mumps. "No need to worry, though. JoAnne Russell stepped in to pick up where Smith left off," according to a *Supertiebreaker* article.

But the San Diego Friars did ultimately take a match off Dallas in a close battle.

"The Stars' Steve Denton and Kevin Curren beat Butch Walts and Ross Case 6-4 in the first set. Denton then whipped Walts 6-1, giving the Stars a comfortable 12-5 lead," according to a match report.

"Mary Lou Piatek and Anne White then edged JoAnne Russell and Sharon Walsh 7-6," according to the match report. But Piatek knew the match was within grasp for her team, beating Russell 6-2. Next, Piatek continued her form by partnering with Ross Case to defeat Curren and Walts 6-3. The score? 24-23 for the Friars.

"It would be the last defeat Dallas would suffer," according to a *Supertiebreaker* explaining the match. "The Stars topped Phoenix, the eventual runners-up, 33-23 in Phoenix. The Chicago Aces lost by three, and then Los Angeles paid its dues for handing Dallas its first loss and fell 23-20."

The season rundown continued, "In the last regular season game, Dallas beat Oakland by five in tuning up for the Championship against Phoenix."

The final match of the 1982 season went like this using traditional scoring in tennis: "Curren and Walsh started things off with a 6-2 win over Pam Teeguarden and Tom Gullikson," according to the match report. "Gullikson then came back to beat Steve Denton 6-2 to even things up. Teeguarden and Ann Kiyomura took Walsh and Russell to the brink 7-6 before winning...Russell bounced back to beat Teeguarden 7-5, and Denton and Curren sealed the victory with a 6-2 triumph over Andrew Pattison and Gullikson."

**

The third season since WTT's revival, 1984, was a historic one on a number of levels. First, it had the Los Angeles Olympics to contend with and thus needed to change the structure yet again to cope. For instance, instead of continuing with its three-week season as before, the league switched over to a one-week knockout tournament.

Billie Jean King competed for the Chicago Fyre ahead of becoming the league's commissioner. King's last season on the WTT court was with this 1984 Fyre squad. Pictured (l. to r.): Trey Waltke, Billie Jean King, Sharon Walsh-Pete and Ben Testerman. Photo: World TeamTennis

But even more importantly for the league and its future, Billie Jean King became the commissioner. In doing so, she became the first female commissioner of a professional sports league, once again serving as a role model for women in sports and a trailblazer in her own right.

In an article called, "The Time is Right," Tom Bonk captured the essence of King's role as commissioner of the league. "You can't really place Billie Jean King in any one time frame. That would be wrong. King is as much a part of the future as TeamTennis promises to be under her leadership."

He added: "Commissioner King? Yes, that's what TeamTennis has come to, and it's a good thing, too. Who could be better to lead the sport of tennis in bold, new directions than King, who has been doing it her entire career."

"We are a sport whose time really is right now," she said. "It's different. It's more social. It's more fun."

"We're going to take longer to make it," King continued in an interview at the time. "But we're going to be solid."

She continued with an understanding that the league wouldn't change drastically immediately, but rather require dedication and persistence. "We're not going to have a big splash overnight, but we're going to build in a constructive way."

And to that effect, King said that the owners are of utmost importance for the league's growth. The owners of the various franchises need to be committed to the league's future, she expressed.

"The owners are the backbone of TeamTennis," she said. "Our owners love tennis and are really involved in the community."

King added: "That was absolutely imperative for TeamTennis. We want—and have—owners who run their teams like a business instead of a hobby."

"Billie Jean is a dynamite lady and no one could have gotten me involved in this other than her," said Leo Rose, the owner of the San Antonio team in an interview.

Roy Eisenhardt, the owner of the Oakland Aces and another fan of the King's work over the years, also praised her in an interview with *Supertiebreaker*.

"She certainly is the driving force behind the league," he explained.

***

The league also celebrated 10 years since its first season.

"Ten years ago, a new sport was introduced to the nation's sports fans," Mitch Chortkoff wrote in the *Santa Monica Evening Outlook* to celebrate the team's decade anniversary. "For the first time, tennis players would represent teams. For the first time, the scores of their matches would count toward an overall total." He added: "Everyone admitted one thing—it was sure different. And good."

Chortkoff looked ahead to the league's future, describing the changes with the league over the years from its version spanning over a few months in the '70s to its revival for the three-week events and then the Olympic version of just a week.

"I've covered a lot of events during my years as a sportswriter," he continued. "I've seen few where the participants are so enthusiastic." After all, the journalist added, Vijay Amritraj was such a fan of the format that he "volunteered to sell tickets around Marina del Rey," where was living.

Chortkoff spoke to Billie Jean King for the article, too, in honor of her league's 10th year since starting. The newly minted commissioner, of course, was happy with the league's progress at the time and hopeful for its future.

"We're the healthiest we've been in the 1980s," she said. "Our concept has been accepted."

He also wrote about how the league was attracting strong players through its annual draft. "The point is," explained Chortkoff, "there's no absence of talent." But he was also critical and skeptical of the league's future in direct contrast to King's optimism. "I don't know if TeamTennis will ever return to the days when the biggest names played and huge arenas were filled," he wrote. "I do know there's a market for it. When so many people, including players, fans, and even sportswriters, like something so much it has a real chance."

After all, in its earliest days, WTT attracted thousands to watch players compete, as he mentioned in his rundown of the league's history. For instance, take the year 1978, when the Strings played the Boston Lobsters in a best-of-five playoff for the championship.

According to Chortkoff, "A crowd of 10,000 came to the Forum but the Strings lost the match. Now it was down to one match for the title," he explained. "There was no chance to sell tickets in advance. It was strictly a walk-up crowd."

But people showed up in droves. "To illustrate how TeamTennis had caught on with the L.A. fans, almost 8,000 were out for that final match," he explained. There were also the times in 1976, he wrote, when a match between Phoenix and Pittsburgh drew 13,492 fans.

With those examples, Chortkoff proclaimed that WTT had huge drawing power and a fan base that wanted more and never to see it go away. "Even when the sport had its greatest problems it didn't fade away. There were always people who remembered the pleasure it brought," he added. "There was always someone to bring it back."

***

Highlight #2: Billie Jean King Takes the Reins

Over the years, Billie Jean King has never been one to shy away from expressing her belief in the philosophy of World TeamTennis. "What I like, philosophically, is the socialization of men's and women's sports," she said in the '80s about the league. "Having men and women on the same team is a really good idea. It's interesting that in TeamTennis, men and women can contribute equally."

She added, "Every game you win for your team, whether you're a man or a woman, doesn't really matter by gender."

King stopped playing after her 1984 season in order to switch over completely to her duties as commissioner of World TeamTennis. "So we'll see how it goes, this idea of TeamTennis. Eight teams play 14 matches to divide up $400,000. Those are the numbers, but they represent only part of the reality because the numbers are going to change," said *Supertiebreaker*. "More teams and more money. But the reality, as far as Billie Jean King is concerned, is a bit more involved and personal."

Why? Because she wouldn't be playing anymore, but rather was even more focused on the league's future as commissioner and as a supporter since the very beginning. "That will be another first for her, of course [not playing], but then she's not going to be just sitting around," added the *Supertiebreaker* write-up. "She's got to make this thing work. She's just got to if you listen to her."

Indeed, she appeared as optimistic for the future as ever. "Career-wise and time-wise, I was really coming to an end, so this is right for me," said King.

"I want to spend 95 percent of my time on TeamTennis," she added. "I think it's the only way we are ever going to make tennis a huge spectator sport."

"The work we are doing now probably won't be appreciated until two or three years from now," said King. "But we're doing things right. People are going to know we are solid. Getting the right owners and Domino's Pizza sponsorship are the two most important elements," she continued at the time.

King also highlighted that the league was going in a new direction: it was starting recreational league programs in order to teach men, women, and children the format in clubs and schools across the country.

"We've got to get people who really care. They are interested in their communities and the grassroots program that will be set up in conjunction with Domino's Pizza."

As the *Supertiebreaker* article concluded, "You can take it from a woman who has always been ahead of her time." It continued: "The future of TeamTennis starts right now, and Billie Jean King wants to make sure you don't miss a single second of it."

***

In 1983, the Chicago Fyre proved the strongest team around, with Billie Jean King claiming the title and with the team winning all their home matches. Meanwhile, it was coached by Ilana Kloss, a No. 1 in doubles from South Africa who had played in the very first season of WTT. That would be King's third WTT title and Kloss' one and only. Meanwhile, King played the next year with the Chicago Fyre before switching fully to her role as commissioner of the league.

The San Diego Buds claimed the title in 1984, an Olympic year, as well as in 1985. Pictured (l. to r.): Butch Walts, Mary Lou Piatek-Daniels, Robin White, Todd Nelson and coach Larry Willens (far right) along with his son Richard. Photo: World TeamTennis

The next year in 1984, the San Diego Buds claimed the title during the Olympics year by taking part in the one-week long tournament. They beat out five other teams to take the title.

Then, the year after, in 1985, it was the Buds again who took out their competition, beating the St. Louis Slims 25-24 in San Antonio.

WTT FINALS 1981

Los Angeles Strings
Champion determined by
Regular Season Record

WTT FINALS 1982

Dallas Stars 27

Phoenix Sunsets 22

WTT FINALS 1983

Chicago Fyre 26

Los Angeles Strings 20

WTT FINALS **1984**

San Diego Buds
Season consisted of
one-week tournament.

WTT FINALS **1985**

San Diego Buds 25

St. Louis Slims 24

Chapter Three: Seasons Eleven to Fifteen (1986-1990):

A Legacy Grows

1986 TEAMS & PLAYERS:

Boston Bays:	Owen Davidson, Andrea Jaeger, Paula Smith, Butch Walts. COACH: Owen Davidson
Chicago Fire:	John Mattke, Leif Shiras, Molly Van Nostrand, Yvonne Vermaak. COACH: Mike Kernodle
Corpus Christi Advantage:	Sandy Collins, Dave Dowlen, Ann Henricksson, Terry Moor. COACH: Chris Crawford
Los Angeles Strings:	Penny Barg, Lisa Bonder, Steve Meister, Eliot Teltscher. COACH: Lornie Kuhle
Miami Beach Breakers:	Rosie Casals, Tim Gullickson, Susan Mascarin, Ilie Nastase. COACH: Ilie Nastase
Oakland Aces:	Mike DePalmer Jr., Chris Dunk, Peanut Louie, Sharon Walsh. COACH: Lynne Rolley
Sacramento Capitals:	Pam Casale, Mary Lou Piatek-Daniels, Larry Stefanki, Robert Van't Hof. COACH: Larry Willens
San Antonio Racquets:	Candy Reynolds, Anne Smith, Ben Testerman, Kim Warwick. COACH: Clarence Mabry
WTT FINALS *(in San Antonio, Texas):*	San Antonio Racquets def. Sacramento Capitals 25-23

1987 TEAMS & PLAYERS:

Charlotte Heat:	Mike DePalmer Jr., Elna Reinach, Monica Reinach, John Sadri. COACH: Karl Coombes
Los Angeles Strings:	Lisa Bonder, John Lloyd, Eliot Teltscher, Anne White. COACH: John Lloyd
Miami Beach Breakers:	Sandy Collins, Laura Gildemeister, Heinz Gunthardt, Andy Kohlberg, Matt Mitchell. COACH: Virginia Brown
New Jersey Stars:	Colin Dibley, Hank Pfister, Joanne Russell, Molly Van Nostrand. COACH: Colin Dibley
Sacramento Capitals:	Pam Casale, Mary Lou Piatek-Daniels, Larry Stefanki, Robert Van't Hof. COACH: Larry Willens

San Antonio Racquets:	Gary Donnelly, Eric Korita, Gretchen Magers, Anne Smith, Kim Warwick. COACH: Clarence Mabry
WTT FINALS *(in Charlotte, N.C.)*:	Charlotte Heat def. San Antonio Racquets 25-20

1988 TEAMS & PLAYERS:

Charlotte Heat:	Eddie Edwards, Elna Reinach, Monica Reinach, Tim Wilkison. COACH: Karl Coombes
Fresno Sun-Nets:	Rosie Casals, Sandy Collins, Francisco Gonzalez, John Letts. COACH: Peter Doerner
Los Angeles Strings:	Penny Barg, Elise Burgin, John Lloyd, Leif Shiras
New Jersey Stars:	Jenny Byrne, Belinda Cordwell, Peter Fleming, Matt Mitchell. COACH: Peter Fleming
Portland Panthers:	Dianne Balestrat, Marcel Freeman, Andy Kohlberg, Sharon Walsh Pete. COACH: Mike Tammen
Sacramento Capitals:	Ricardo Acuna, Mary Lou Piatek-Daniels, Barbara Gerken, Robert Van't Hof. COACH: Larry Willens
San Antonio Racquets:	Beverly Bowes, Eric Korita, Nduka Odizor, Candy Reynolds. COACH: Clarence Mabry
South Florida Breakers:	Horacio de la Pena, Heather Ludloff, Susan Mascarin, Blaine Willenborg. COACH: Gary Kesl
WTT FINALS *(in Charlotte, N.C.)*:	Charlotte Heat def. New Jersey Stars 27-22

1989 TEAMS & PLAYERS:

Charlotte Heat:	Cammy MacGregor, Cynthia MacGregor, Larry Stefanki, Sherwood Stewart. COACH: Sherwood Stewart
Fresno Sun-Nets:	Clinton Banducci, Sandy Collins, Jean-Philippe Fleurian, Elly Hakami. COACH: Virginia Brown
Los Angeles Strings:	Lise Gregory, John Lloyd, Anne Minter, Roger Smith. COACH: John Lloyd
New Jersey Stars:	John Austin, Tracy Austin, Bill Scanlon, Shaun Stafford, Leigh Thompson. COACH: Asim Sengun
Portland Panthers:	Mike DePalmer Jr., Andy Kohlberg, Ronnie Reis, Anne Smith, Mike Tammen. COACH: Mike DePalmer Sr.
Sacramento Capitals:	Sophie Amiach, Greg Holmes, Molly Van Nostrand, Robert Van't Hof. COACH: Larry Willens
San Antonio Racquets:	Gary Donnelly, Eddie Edwards, Elna Reinach, Monica Reinach. COACH: Karl Coombes

Wellington Aces:	Penny Barg, Heather Ludloff, Joey Rive, Blaine Willenborg. COACH: Andy Brandi
WTT FINALS *(in Sacramento, Calif.):*	San Antonio Racquets def. Sacramento Capitals 27-25

1990 TEAMS & PLAYERS:
EAST DIVISION:

Charlotte Heat:	Donna Faber, Paul Koscielski, Trevor Kronemann, Ronni Reis. COACH: Jim Boykin
Miami Beach Breakers:	Sandy Collins, Cammy MacGregor, Francisco Montana, Richard Schmidt, Greg Van Emburgh. COACH: Virginia Brown
New Jersey Stars:	Shane Barr, John Sullivan, Janine Thompson, Linda Harvey-Wild. COACH: Phil Atkinson
Raleigh Edge:	Beth Herr, Tim Pawsat, Shaun Stafford, Tim Wilkison. COACH: Jimmy Corn
Wellington Aces:	Rick Brown, Jenny Byrne, Heather Ludloff, Scott Warner. COACH: Bobby Blair

WEST DIVISION:

Los Angeles Strings:	Nick Brown, John Lloyd, Larry Stefanki, Anne White, Robin White. COACH: John Lloyd
Newport Beach Dukes:	Sophie Amiach, Marty Davis, Amy Frazier, Roger Smith. COACH: Greg Patton
Sacramento Capitals:	Maria Lindstrom, Michiel Schapers, Robert Van't Hof, Tami Whitlinger. COACH: Dave Borelli
San Antonio Racquets:	Dacio Campos, Mary Lou Piatek-Daniels, Elna Reinach, Sammy Giammalva. COACH: Bob McKinley
WTT FINALS *(in Los Angeles, Calif.):*	Los Angeles Strings def. Raleigh Edge 27-16

With Billie Jean King firmly in command of the league and the sponsorship of Domino's Pizza locked in for at least another year, World TeamTennis found itself poised to grow—and thrive—with newfound security for the first time in years. The Olympics were over, a fearless leader was in place, and there were teams taking shape with committed owners to ensure another competitive season after the San Diego Buds secured their two-peat, a first in the league's history in consecutive years, over the St. Louis Slims.

Moreover, the league held a newly minted position of not only establishing itself as a professional sports league but also as an organization committed to growing a recreational league for tennis players of all ages and abilities, thanks to its sponsor's guidance and support.

The recreational portion began in 1985 with the new sponsorship, which King wrote about in her 1985 letter to fans in the year's *Supertiebreaker* magazine.

"Domino's Pizza TeamTennis was created to allow equal opportunity for both men and women and boys and girls to work together in team competition," she wrote. "Our goal is to have all levels of Domino's Pizza TeamTennis play; from grassroots to the professional ranks, including national adult leagues."

To that effect, 1986 saw the addition of two staff members responsible for the growth of the league's new recreationally focused branch: Delaine Mast and Elaine Wingfield. After the first year, there were already 150 leagues playing with the WTT format in 1986, according to Sarah Edwards in an article written about its expansion.

Notably, the year also saw the first collegiate competition held whereby students at U.S. universities enjoyed the chance to compete using the league's signature format.

"It all started last year with a professional league," a *Supertiebreaker* article at the time began, "then in the fall, with a recreational league, and now for the first time ever Domino's Pizza TeamTennis has entered the world of collegiate tennis."

The first event was held at Duke University's west campus in April, according to the article. Then four Atlantic Coast Conference co-ed teams competed in the historic tournament. The teams involved: Duke University, the University of North Carolina at Chapel Hill, Wake Forest University, and North Carolina State University.

"Coming out on top were the Duke Blue Devils after defeating the Wolfpack of North Carolina State University in the finals," it continued.

"We had a lot of fun using the Domino's Pizza TeamTennis format," John LeBar, the winning coach from Duke, said after his team's victory. "The...format provided excitement for both the spectators and players."

"I enjoyed playing," Brandon Tise from Wake Forest, added. "It was fun having your own team cheer you on, where in regular tennis everyone is busy playing their own matches at the same time."

He continued, "It provided more camaraderie amongst my teammates."

As the recreational league continued in the next years, it expanded enormously. The league stated that in just three years, and by the 1987 season, "the leagues have flourished across the country with more than 55,000 participants in more than 500 cities."

The article continued, "Players of all ages and abilities are joining teams year round at public parks, tennis clubs, schools, military bases, and residential communities."

The Charlotte Heat were the league's 1987 champions. Pictured (l. to r.): John Sadri, Monica Reinach, Coach Karl Coombes, Elna Reinach and Mike DePalmer Jr. Photo: World TeamTennis

Ilana Kloss, who by the 1987 season had been promoted to executive director to lead the league alongside King, said at the time: "We want to make tennis fun for everyone. Our format is social, it's competitive, and it's easy to administer for recreational players."

And to help grow it, Commissioner King explained that it followed the format of a popular pastime for youngsters. "For the sport of tennis to grow, it has to be organized at the local level like Little League baseball and soccer."

To help the league's recreational experience grow that season, WTT executives did a little grassroots organizing on their own in order to promote it. "To bring national and local awareness to recreational tennis players and programs, Domino's Pizza TeamTennis undertook an unprecedented 15-city tour in the spring of this year," according to the season's official magazine. "Highlights of the tour included a visit to Ft. Bragg army base in Fayetteville, N.C., and involvement with Fresno, California's model USTA schools program."

But it also held personal significance for King, a native of California. "The tour also brought Billie Jean back home to play on the public courts in Long Beach, California where she first learned the game," the article continued. "It was the first time in nearly 20 years that she had played on those courts."

In fact, this was the clinic during which Billie Jean King met Serena and Venus Williams for the first time. To make the event even more special, King's "homecoming" included Los Angeles Strings player and coach, John Lloyd, taking part in the events planned for the day. There were other events held throughout the country, including in Florida with a collegiate event, USTA events, and a Chicago charity event for a local hospital.

***

Highlight #3: WTT Rec League takes tennis to the people

Recreational league players from around the country travel to the WTT Nationals to battle for national division championships each fall. Photo: World TeamTennis

The recreational WTT branch for players across the country started in the mid-'80s as a result of the partnership with Domino's Pizza. To that effect, the league hired two women to initially help run the program: Delaine Mast and Elaine Wingfield.

Both women worked for the league for nearly 30 years, beginning in 1986. Over that time, the recreational league has inspired over one million men, women, and children to take part in the WTT format, according to Mast's calculation from 2015.

"We literally are growing the game of tennis. And it's following Billie's philosophy of men and women working together equally on the same team," said Mast.

With over 100 events run per year, Mast said that she's been able to experiment with the format and to try innovative practices under the guidance of King and Ilana Kloss. "What keeps me going and gets me excited is that they are always willing to try new things," she said. "They are always willing to listen, and even if they don't agree with something we want to do, most of the time they'll let us try it and see whether or not it'll work."

Mast discussed the start of Tennis on Campus, a program Wingfield works on today. "The reason that it's as successful as it is today because it's always been a team effort," she explained about the program, which is a collaboration with the USTA. "It was all something that we worked on as a team. We collaborated on as a group."

She also emphasized the skills that the recreational league teaches children. "You want the nine, ten, eleven, twelve-year-old kids to learn that they can play tennis as a team sport," said Mast. "To learn that they can root their teammates on, to learn that they can sit on the sidelines and cheer them is just as much an important part of the game as it is when you're in hitting the ball. To learn to work together."

For Wingfield, World TeamTennis was an easy transition from her days at Ohio State. In fact, she actually played in the format during the '70s when there was a collegiate tournament held and her team played.

Something that Wingfield said is important to her work with the League is just how nimble the organization can be to exact change and to grow. "We don't have the politics that other organizations have, so if we want to try a rule, we just do it," she explained. "In both the recreational league and the pro league, the pro league it has to go through the owners but they're not afraid to innovate and to try things."

Similar to Mast, the ability to work under King and Kloss has been something special for Wingfield, especially in the promotion of tennis across the United States. For instance, she recalls watching King sign autographs after a match one day. "It's such a kick to watch the autographs," she said. The children "would bring their Billie Jean King Tennis rackets." Wingfield added: "It was just fun to go and see the things that people would bring for Billie to sign. You just forget how long she's been doing it and how many lives she's touched."

And Kloss, too, has been an exceptional leader, according to Wingfield. "Ilana's done such a great job. She knows the issues that Billie wants to push forward with tennis and she's been great for the game and for Billie."

***

The pro league for the 1986 season saw eight teams compete for the trophy. They were: the Boston Bays, owned by Alan Morell of IMG; the Oakland Aces, owned by Roy Eisenhardt; the Corpus Christi Advantage, owned by Bob Eagle; the Los Angeles Strings, owned by Jerry Buss; the Miami Beach Breakers, owned by Javier Holtz; the Sacramento Capitals, owned by Richard Benvenuti; the San Antonio Racquets, owned by Leo Rose; and the Chicago Fyre, owned by Bill and Barbara Schoen. At the conclusion of the month-long season, it was the San Antonio Racquets who claimed victory over the Sacramento Capitals with a 25-23 win in San Antonio.

***

In 1987, the last two teams standing were the Charlotte Heat and the San Antonio Racquets, the defending champions, who once again found themselves in the league finals. The energy in the crowd was booming with 5,000 people packed into the stadium holding the event in Charlotte, North Carolina. In fact, there were so many people clamoring to get a look at the two teams playing that it was standing room only.

The teams quickly proved why they had made it out of their semifinal matches. At the final four stage, the Heat defeated the Sacramento Capitals, who were last year's finalists, by a slim margin: 24-23. Meanwhile, San Antonio, the defending champions, took out the Miami Beach Breakers by a wider margin of 29-21.

Charlotte took the lead early thanks to the strategy employed by the team's coach, Karl Coombes, and the league's MVP, Elna Reinach, who won the mixed doubles with her teammate Mike DePalmer. She followed it up with a singles win to nab her team a 12-8 lead.

But the Racquets wouldn't be pushed aside that easily. After all, they had Rookie of the Year Eric Korita on their team, who won men's doubles and singles to grab the momentum back for his players with a 20-19 lead.

"Coombes had opted for Women's Doubles to be the fifth set. After all, he had the league's top tandem in Reinach sisters—Elna and Monica," according to an article about the finals. "Yet the Racquets had the veteran duo of Anne Smith and Gretchen Magers, the league's No. 2 team who had finished only a few percentage points behind the Reinachs during the regular season."

And not only that, but the two teams split their previous meetings leading up to the championship match, "and now the entire championship rested on the shoulders of these four stars as they walked out onto the court."

"Coombes must have known something as the Reinachs played flawlessly," the article continued, "blistering the Texans, 6-0 to take the title for the Heat 25-20."

And whatever he was doing was obviously working. In 1988, his team reached the league finals for the second straight year. This time, their opponents were the New Jersey Stars. The teams faced off against one another in blistering heat that saw the court reach temperatures of 120 degrees under the summer sun in Sacramento, California

That season the eight teams in contention for the title were the Heat, South Florida Breakers, Stars, Sacramento Capitals, Portland Panthers, San Antonio Racquets, Los Angeles Strings and the Fresno Sun-Nets.

In 1988, the team was even more dominant than in the previous one. Consisting of Elna and Monica Reinach, Tim Wilkison, Eddie Edwards, and Coach Karl Coombes, they went 12-2 during the season, while also claiming three of the five individual events in terms of performance over the other athletes.

"Elna Reinach topped both the Women's Singles and Mixed Doubles (w/Edwards) standings, and Wilkison dominated the Men's Singles," according to the match report. "Edwards and Wilkison also finished second in Men's Doubles behind South Florida's de la Pena and Willenborg. The Star's Byrne and Cordwell captured the top spot in the Women's Doubles overall standings."

In the semis, the Stars took out the Breakers 30-15, while the Heat once again had a close call against the Sacramento Capitals. They beat them 25-23 to advance. Notably, the Stars were totally different from their 1987 squad. In that season, they finished with an 0-14 record and just a year later found themselves playing the defending championship with a 9-5 season record.

But with the championship set for August 6 on Saturday night, it simply wasn't to be, because of a thunderstorm that totally washed out the match. The crowd, however, returned the next day to witness it.

"The Stars, who had seized the first set, men's doubles, only to fall behind 22-14 after losing women's singles, women's doubles, and men's singles, came back strong in the final set with Fleming and Byrne defeating Elna Reinach and Eddie Edwards in mixed doubles, 6-4, to force play into extended play."

There, New Jersey carried the momentum until Coach Coombes substituted Wilkison with Edwards. In their first substitution of the season, according to the match report, they won the very next game to take the match and title, 27-22.

***

The 1989 season saw the San Antonio Racquets face off against Sacramento in the finals. To get there, the Racquets upset the regular season top finisher, the New Jersey Stars, in the playoff match.

"The San Antonio team of Elna and Monica Reinach, Eddie Edwards, and Gary Donnelly struggled to a fourth place (7-7) showing in the regular season," according to the official match report for the championship. However, they weren't to be dismissed by the league's top teams that season. "They came on strong in the playoffs defeating New Jersey in the semi-finals, 28-19."

But the team wasn't new to winning. In fact, Karl Coombes, the coach for the Racquets, had just led the Charlotte team and switched over, taking Edwards and the Reinach sisters with him. Meanwhile, to advance to the semis, Sacramento defeated the Portland Panthers in a tight 26-25 win.

"The male and female playoff MVPs, Edwards and Elna Reinach, were the difference for the Racquets in the championship match," according to the article. "The two teamed to give San Antonio an early lead when they upset the top mixed doubles team of Robert van't Hoff and Molly Van Nostrand, 6-3, in the first event."

The next set saw a surge by Sacramento as Sophie Amiach rallied to get her team back in action by taking out Elna Reinach, 6-5. "The Racquets nearly put the match away in women's doubles with the Reinach sisters winning five straight games," the report continued. "However, Amiach and Van Nostrand came back to win four straight games before falling 6-4." Men's singles saw Greg Holmes and Donnelly battle it out, with Holmes winning to give San Antonio a slight 21-19 edge heading into the final set.

"With the support of the hometown fans urging them on, Sacramento's van't Hoff and Holmes defeated Donnelly and Edwards to win the men's doubles 6-5 to force the match into Overtime with San Antonio leading 26-25," according to the article.

And with Edwards able to hold his serve, the Racquets claimed the championship for the 1989 season of WTT.

"It was pretty nerve-wracking," said Elna Reinach after the match. "We were never sure we would win until the final point."

Ilana Kloss, who was the vice president of the league at the time, praised the depth of the field during the season and especially at the championship match. "Looking at the standings and prize money list, one can see how competitive the matches were and how much depth there was," she said after the match ended. "The five individual events were won by players on five different teams. Attendance was up across the board."

Kloss continued, "We're very happy with the success of the 1989 season."

***

TeamTennis celebrated its 10 anniversary in 1990, and the league celebrated a few big milestones. Along with there being $450,000 offered for the players to win during the professional league play, the recreational branch of the league also blossomed. In fact, by the end of the year, the league boasted having 165,000 participants by the end of the year with play in over 1,000 cities.

The Los Angeles Strings defeated the Raleigh Edge to claim the 1990 title. Pictured (l. to r.): Team GM Jeanie Buss, player/coach John Lloyd, Anne White, Nick Brown, Robin White, Larry Stefanki and WTT co-founder Billie Jean King. Photo: World TeamTennis

Meanwhile, nine teams competed in two divisions, with six of those vying for their very first WTT title.

"This is an exciting year for TeamTennis," said CEO Billie Jean King ahead of the season. "We have nine years of history on which we can look back, but we have not even put a dent into the history we are going to make in 1990 and beyond," she said in a *Supertiebreaker* interview.

The Los Angeles String were the dominant force during the season with player and coach John Lloyd named the season's Coach of the Year and Robin White named the Female Player of the Year.

To make it to the finals, Los Angeles beat out the West Division, leading throughout the regular season. In the Eastern Divisional Semis, the Charlotte Heat and Miami Beach Breakers played one another.

"In a match that went down to the last game, Miami Beach edged the Heat 25-24, to advance to the Eastern Divisional Finals in Raleigh," according to the match report. "The Edge beat the Breakers, 27-17, to advance from the Eastern Division into the 1990 Championship match."

Meanwhile, for the Western Divisional Semis, San Antonio and Sacramento faced off, while the Racquets beat the Capitals 28-17 in the other match. "The Strings advanced to the Championship match by beating San Antonio, 24-18, in the Western Division Finals."

There, Los Angeles quickly asserted itself as the team to beat once again by snatching an early lead. They never looked back either and claimed a 27-16 lopsided victory for the title, a first since the league restarted in 1981 after its brief hiatus.

"It capped an incredible season for the Strings who finished at 14-2 tying a record set by Charlotte in 1987," according to the article. "Nine years after winning its first title, Los Angeles had won its second title."

It continued, "It's tough to beat a team with history on its side."

WTT FINALS 1986

San Antonio Racquets 25

Sacramento Capitals 23

WTT FINALS 1987

Charlotte Heat 25

San Antonio Racquets 20

WTT FINALS 1988

Charlotte Heat 27

New Jersey Stars 22

WTT FINALS 1989

San Antonio Racquets 27

Sacramento Capitals 25

WTT FINALS 1990

Los Angeles Strings 27

Raleigh Edge 16

Chapter Four: Seasons Sixteen to Twenty (1991-1995):

WTT Turns Twenty

1991 TEAMS & PLAYERS:

EAST DIVISION:

Atlanta Thunder:	Marty Davis, Mariaan de Swardt, Kelly Evernden, Martina Navratilova. COACH: Craig Kardon
Charlotte Heat:	Mike DePalmer Jr., Ginger Helgeson Nielsen, Trevor Kronemann, Candy Reynolds, Tami Whitlinger. COACH: Ed Krass
Miami Breakers:	Matt Anger, Beverly Bowes, Sandy Collins, Greg Holmes. COACH: Virginia Brown
New Jersey Stars:	Ann Grossman, Leif Shiras, Larry Stefanki, Rennae Stubbs. COACH: Phil Atkinson
Raleigh Edge:	Todd Nelson, Ronni Reis, Pat Serrett, Shaun Stafford, Tim Wilkison. COACH: Dan Weant
Wellington Aces:	Will Bull, Heather Ludloff, Stacey Schefflin, Richard Schmidt. COACH: Bobby Blair

WEST DIVISION:

Los Angeles Strings:	Jimmy Connors, Mary Lou Piatek-Daniels, John Lloyd, Robin White. COACH: John Lloyd
Newport Beach Dukes:	Amy Frazier, Manon Bollegraf, Elise Burgin, Rick Leach, Jorge Lozano, Tim Pawsat. COACH: Greg Patton
Sacramento Capitals:	Kelly Jones, Alysia May, Robert Van't Hof, Tami Whitlinger, Teri Whitlinger. COACH: Dave Borelli
San Antonio Racquets:	Louise Allen, Linda Barnard, Peter Doohan, Sammy Giammalva, Gretchen Magers, Anne Smith. COACH: Bob McKinley
Wichita Advantage:	Buff Farrow, Craig Johnson, Cammy MacGregor, Catherine Suire. COACH: Mervyn Webster
WTT FINALS (in Atlanta, Ga.):	Atlanta Thunder def. Los Angeles Strings 27-16

1992 TEAMS & PLAYERS:
EAST DIVISION:

Atlanta Thunder:	Kelly Evernden, Heather Ludloff, Martina Navratilova, Brett Steven. COACH: Craig Kardon
New Jersey Stars:	Ann Grossman, Matt Lucena, Rennae Stubbs. Player/COACH: Larry Stefanki
Raleigh Edge:	Mike DePalmer Jr., Shannan McCarthy, Chanda Rubin. Player/COACH: Tim Wilkison
San Antonio Racquets:	Louise Allen, Jean-Philippe Fleurian, Ginger Helgeson Nielsen, Trevor Kronemann. COACH: Bob McKinley
Tampa Bay Action:	Jill Hetherington, Mikael Pernfors, Kathy Rinaldi, Tobias Svantesson. COACH: Bobby Blair

WEST DIVISION:

Los Angeles Strings:	Jimmy Connors, Carrie Cunningham, Mary Lou Piatek-Daniels. Player/COACH: John Lloyd
Sacramento Capitals:	Debbie Graham, Steve DeVries, Patty Fendick, David MacPherson. COACH: Robert Van't Hof
Vail Eagles:	Sandy Collins, Scott Davis, Lori McNeil, David Pate, Shaun Stafford. COACH: Virginia Brown
Wichita Advantage:	Buff Farrow, Cammy MacGregor, Craig Johnson, Stella Sampras. COACH: Mervyn Webster
Newport Beach Dukes:	Katrina Adams, Ronnie Bathman, Rikard Bergh, Amy Frazier, Lise Gregory. COACH: Greg Patton
Phoenix Smash:	Rosalyn Fairbank-Nideffer, Ellis Ferreira, Greg Holmes, Kelly Evernden, Anne Smith. COACH: Andrew Pattison
WTT FINALS (in Atlanta, Ga.):	Atlanta Thunder def. Newport Beach Dukes 30-17

1993 TEAMS & PLAYERS:
EAST DIVISION:

Atlanta Thunder:	Kelly Evernden, Heather Ludloff, Cassio Motta, Martina Navratilova. COACH: Craig Kardon
Florida Twist:	Nicole Arendt, Jimmy Arias, Paul Kilderry, Iva Majoli. COACH: Jose Lambert
Kansas City Explorers:	Ken Flach, Brent Haygarth, Gretchen Magers, Marianne Werdel. COACH: Paul Smith
New Jersey Stars:	Jenny Byrne, Mariaan De Swardt, Mats Wilander. Player/COACH: Ronnie Bathman
Raleigh Edge:	Tracy Austin, Neil Broad, Sandy Collins, Player/COACH: Tim Wilkison
Wichita Advantage:	Buff Farrow, Lori McNeil, T.J. Middleton, Julie Steven, Substitute: Jennifer Santrock. COACH: Mervyn Webster

WEST DIVISION:

Los Angeles Strings:	Bjorn Borg, Kimberly Po, Robin White, Player/COACH: Larry Stefanki
Minnesota Penguins:	Paul Annacone, Jessica Emmons, Ginger Helgeson Nielsen, Johan Kriek. COACH: Barry Lewis
Newport Beach Dukes:	Katrina Adams, Rikard Bergh, Manon Bollegraf, Trevor Kronemann, Substitutes: Amy Frazier, Zina Garrison-Jackson. COACH: Greg Patton
Phoenix Smash:	Jimmy Connors, Carrie Cunningham, Mary Lou Piatek-Daniels, Ellis Ferreira. COACH: John Lloyd
Sacramento Capitals:	Lindsay Davenport, Steve DeVries, Patty Fendick, David MacPherson. COACH: Robert Van't Hof
San Antonio Racquets:	Cammy MacGregor, Sven Salumaa, Shaun Stafford, Andrew Sznajder. COACH: Bob McKinley
WTT FINALS (in Atlanta, Ga.):	Wichita Advantage def. Newport Beach Dukes 26-23

1994 TEAMS & PLAYERS:
EAST DIVISION:

Atlanta Thunder:	Bjorn Borg, Kelly Evernden, Chandra Rubin, Dinky Van Rensburg. COACH: Ashley Rhoney
Charlotte Express:	Jenny Byrne, Johan Kriek, Mercedes Paz, Byron Talbot. COACH: Karl Coombes
Florida Twist:	Nicole Arendt, Andres Gomez, Kristine Radford, Greg Van Emburgh. COACH: Mike DePalmer, Sr.
New Jersey Stars:	John-Laffnie de Jager, Mariaan de Swardt, Brian Devening, Martina Navratilova. COACH: Craig Kardon

CENTRAL DIVISION:

Kansas City Explorers:	Jill Hetherington, Luke Jensen, Murphy Jensen, Shaun Stafford. COACH: Paul Smith
San Antonio Racquets:	Jonathan Canter, Caroline Kuhlman, Elna Reinach, Christo van Rensburg. COACH: Bob McKinley
St. Louis Aces:	Ken Flach, Brent Haygarth, Patricia Hy, Julie Richardson. COACH: Rick Flach
Wichita Advantage:	Buff Farrow, Lori McNeil, T.J. Middleton, Julie Steven. COACH: Mervyn Webster

WEST DIVISION:

Idaho Sneakers:	Manon Bollegraf, Amy Frazier, Jon Leach, Rick Leach. COACH: Greg Patton
Newport Beach Dukes:	Zina Garrison Jackson, Kelly Jones, Trevor Kronemann, Larisa Neiland. COACH: Angel Lopez

Phoenix Smash:	Jimmy Connors, Mary Lou Piatek-Daniels, Leila Meskhi, Danie Visser. COACH: John Lloyd
Sacramento Capitals:	Debbie Graham, David MacPherson, Kimberly Po, Sandon Stolle. COACH: Robert Van't Hof
WTT FINALS *(in Sacramento, Calif.):*	New Jersey Stars def. Idaho Sneakers 28-25

1995 TEAMS & PLAYERS:
EAST DIVISION:

Atlanta Thunder:	Katrina Adams, Doug Flach, Ken Flach, Linda Harvey-Wild, Zina Garrison-Jackson, Rennae Stubbs. COACH: Tim Noonan
Charlotte Express:	Ann Grossman, Sabine Hack, Stefan Kruger, Christine Neuman, Christine Vickie Paynter, Chanda Rubin, Christo van Rensburg. COACH: Karl Coombes
Florida Twist:	Nicole Arendt, Rikard Bergh, Manon Bollegraf, Kristine Radford, Jimy Szymanski. COACH: Charlton Eagle
New Jersey Stars:	Niklas Kroon, Mariaan de Swardt, Richard Matuszewski, Martina Navratilova, Brad Pearce. COACH: Craig Kardon
New York OTBzz:	Rachel Jensen, Mercedes Paz, Dave Randall, Brenda Schultz, Roger Smith. COACH: Inderjit Singh

WEST DIVISION:

Sacramento Capitals:	Patty Fendick, Trevor Kronemann, Valda Lake, David MacPherson, Natalia Medvedeva, Kimberly Po, Clare Wood. COACH: Robert Van't Hof
St. Louis Aces:	Sandra Cacic, Jonathan Canter, Mary Lou Piatek-Daniels, Larisa Neiland, Ros Nideffer, Bryan Shelton, Pam Shriver, Robin White. COACH: Rick Flach
Wichita Advantage:	Bret Garnett, Elly Hakami, Joannette Kruger, T.J. Middleton, Tara Snyder, Julie Steven. COACH: Mervyn Webster
Idaho Sneakers:	Jane Chi, Amy Frazier, Brett Hansen-Dent, Jon Leach. COACH: Greg Patton
Kansas City Explorers:	Luke Jensen, Murphy Jensen, Rebecca Jensen, Julie Richardson, Shaun Stafford. COACH: Paul Smith
WTT FINALS *(in Charlotte, N.C.):*	New Jersey Stars def. Atlanta Thunder 28-20

If the 1986 to 1990 seasons signified the league's new leadership under Billie Jean King as well as the expansion of recreational leagues spreading the founders' philosophy of equality to the masses, seasons 1991 to 1995 suggested a further established league striving to become a well-oiled machine. It was also marked by the dominance of a couple legendary players: Martina Navratilova and Jimmy Connors.

A large part of the years' success, of course, was Billie Jean's belief in the equality promoted by the new league.

Larry King spoke about just how important it was to her both during WTT's formation and over the years. "Billie Jean likes team tennis for two reasons. One, it allowed you to play in front of a big audience with huge players," he said. "Well, we thought by doing the team concept, we could have ten thousand a night in eight cities and do eighty thousand a night, which is ultimately where we ended up. I mean, we had five million spectators in five years"

King added, "And then secondly, Billie Jean liked the women and men contributing equally to the team's outcome. So, those were the two things that we just thought were automatic winners for Billie Jean, that's the way she always was."

And it certainly got off to a strong start. For the 1991 season, the league expanded to 11 teams, up from nine during its historic 10th season of existence. In her annual letter to fans, Billie Jean King proclaimed proudly news of the robust growth.

"Welcome to the start of the second decade of professional TeamTennis," she began. "With the eleventh season of TeamTennis, we are entering the second stage of growth."

To that effect, she announced some big news for the league's fans: The acquisition of two of the greatest legends of tennis: Martina Navratilova and Jimmy Connors.

***

Highlight #4: Martina Navratilova and Jimmy Connors Join

"Superstar. It's an overused term in athletics," an article in the season's official magazine proclaimed at the onset. "It's an overused term in athletics, but every sport has a few legitimate 'Superstars'— athletes to whom the term truly applies." It continued, "In tennis, two athletes who fit that mold are Martina Navratilova and Jimmy Connors."

As Billie Jean King says, "Real superstars make their teammates better." That's exactly what Navratilova and Connors did when they played WTT.

Jimmy Connors, along with Martina Navratilova, headlined the 1991 season. Photo: World TeamTennis

At the time, they had claimed 26 major singles titles between them, along with over 250 singles titles overall.

"Both Connors and Navratilova raised their sport to new levels. Connors helped popularize tennis in America, he is the kind of athlete that Americans cherish," the article continued, praising their prowess and contextualizing just how important they were to the sport and the league. "It's no coincidence that the tennis boom of the '70's came at the height of Connors' career as young players covered public courts across the country mimicking that legendary grunt."

Navratilova, meanwhile, is worthy of just as many accolades for her dominance of the sport. "Navratilova brought the aggressive serve and volley game to heights never seen before," the *Supertiebreaker* piece read. "She is a true athlete in every sense of the word, and she has been recognized for that fact."

But even more noteworthy to the league, "Connors and Navratilova are now playing TeamTennis and what could suit them better?" the article proclaimed. "Connors the ultimate showman is practically made for the league where player-fan interaction is actually encouraged."

"As for Navratilova, she should thrive in a league where the players play singles, doubles [and mixed doubles] in one match," it added.

"Superstar. It's an overused term in athletics," the announcement concluded. "But in some cases it's a term that fits precisely."

The two champions continued their involvement in the league over the years. And for Connors, TeamTennis played a huge part in his comeback.

According to Cindy Shmerler, the former managing editor of *World Tennis Magazine*: "When Jimmy Connors began the 1991 tennis season he was ranked No. 936 in the world, according to the IBM/ATP Tour computer. The reason for Connors' magnificent plummet out of the world's top 20 following 15 years of Top Ten rankings (including five at No. 1) was a wrist injury that doctors said would force him into retirement."

She added that Connors didn't listen to the doctors. Instead, "six months after returning to the circuit he captured the hearts of most of the sports-loving public by reaching the semifinals of the 1991 US Open." Shmerler continued: "And to what does Connors partially credit his resurgence? TeamTennis."

Navratilova, who crashed out of Wimbledon in 1991 to Jennifer Capriati, who was just fifteen years old at the time, also found her form in time for the U.S. thanks in part to playing in the league.

"While it is impossible to say that Navratilova and Connors would not have had the same success without playing TeamTennis, it is a safe bet that the support two of the sport's all-time greats lend to the team concept went a long way toward making 1991 one of the most talked about seasons in TeamTennis history."

"I love TeamTennis because it's really fast-paced, fast-moving," Navratilova said at the time. "Every point counts because every game counts toward the overall result." She added in an interview: "The crowd really gets into it, you work as a team and you get to play with the guys. For a tennis player who's played hundreds of tournaments, it's a nice change of pace."

"It's New York," said Connors. "It's a US Open kind of atmosphere every time you play and I like that."

For Navratilova, who would go on to become one of the most decorated players ever, WTT was a family for her during her two decades of play in the league. "Martina Navratilova is a true World TeamTennis legend; in fact, no WTT player has played more seasons than Navratilova, and none has garnered as many championship titles," according to the WTT website celebrating her accomplishments over the years. "With 20 seasons and 5 WTT Championship titles under her belt, Navratilova has an impressive list of accolades." Indeed, the list goes on and on, including MVP honors in 1978, 1991, 1992, and 1993. But that's not all she accomplished on the court. She was also the women's scoring leader in 1977, 1978, 1981, 1992, and 1993. To cap off her success, she achieved an honor reserved for a select few to play WTT. "In 2005, Navratilova was named on an elite list: the WTT All-Time All-Star team, comprised of the four best WTT players in the League's history," according to the website.

When Navratilova returned in 2009 for her 20th, and final, season, she also broke another league record as the oldest player to pick up a racquet and compete at 52 years old. Maybe unsurprisingly, she took out players half her age during the season.

Martina Navratilova enjoyed the distinction of being one of the winningest World TeamTennis players during her legendary tennis career. Photo: CameraworkUSA

She attributes her success beyond WTT to her early days with the league. For instance, in 1977, which was her second year with the league, Navratilova had the opportunity to work with coach Roy Emerson as a member of the Boston Lobsters. "Those were my favorite times because I really learned the game. I really got in shape," Navratilova said in an interview.

"Roy Emerson helped me with my strokes, particularly my backhand slice and volley. I actually thanked him for winning my first Wimbledon because I really thought Roy helped me become a better tennis player," she added. "We had so much fun and won a lot of matches. We had great fans in the Walter Brown Arena in Boston."

As one of the smartest players and best tacticians around, Navratilova spoke about the way she competed during her matches. "It was about winning by the biggest margin possible. It wasn't just winning a set; you needed to win by as many games as possible. I was definitely a team player on that front," she said.

"I love that kind of tension, that kind of pressure. Every single game, every single point counted, so I really thrived on that. I broke a few records at the time," Navratilova added. "Quite often, we would give our guys a 10-game lead, which is pretty insurmountable, so the guys were riding on our coattails."

And beyond her own enjoyment from the high-intensity play involved in competing in WTT matches, Navratilova said the league has impacted tennis profoundly over the years. "We had mascots and people really got into it. Those were serious matches and players took it seriously," Navratilova said. "I think it really helped spread the popularity of the sport because we played in cities that didn't normally have tournaments."

"Hopefully, we'll see a longer season and it'll be more worldwide," she continued. "You can only play so many tournaments, but if you have teams playing around the world, you let fans see the sport live and that's a much better product than watching on TV."

***

The season's championship match in 1991 came down to a first-year franchise, the Atlanta Thunder, taking on the defending champions, the Los Angeles Strings. And unsurprisingly, each team had a legend of the sport, with Navratilova belonging to the Thunder, while Connors played for the Strings.

With Navratilova, who last played TeamTennis in 1981 (leading the LA Strings to the championship in its inaugural season), the Thunder dominated the East Division from the outset, ending the regular season with a 12-2 record, far ahead of Charlotte Heat's second place 7-7 finish.

Out West, the Los Angeles team came in second in the regular season but upset the San Antonio Racquets, who went 13-1, in the semis. The Racquets had even secured some records with their play, including the longest regular season winning streak of 13 matches, along with a 7-0 record while traveling. Moreover, the team secured another league first: the most seasons with playoff appearances out of any WTT team in history.

In the semis, Los Angeles took out San Antonio despite their regular season dominance by winning 25-24 to advance to the championship round in a match which ultimately came down to mixed doubles. In the other division final, Atlanta beat Charlotte 30-23.

"While the fury of fan excitement rested clearly on the shoulders of Navratilova and Connors in the championship match," according to the match report, "it was total teamwork that ultimately told the story."

"After Atlanta won the men's doubles 6-5, Connors took the court and disposed of Atlanta's Kelly Evernden 6-3 in men's singles," the report explained. "But Navratilova then displayed some of the magic that earned her TeamTennis titles in women's singles, women's doubles and mixed doubles, not to mention the league's Most Valuable Female player."

She teamed with Marty Davis to take out Los Angeles' John Lloyd and Robin White 6-1 in mixed doubles. Next, in singles, she beat White 6-2. It all ended with Navratilova playing with teammate Mariaan de Swardt to beat White and Mary Lou Daniels 6-2 in women's doubles to secure the victory for the Atlanta Thunder.

The final score: 27-16.

And the victory-thanks to Navratilova's play-also meant a little more history for the team's inaugural victory: the win by an 11-game margin tied the most dominant performance in a championship final since 1990 when the Strings beat Raleigh 27-16 in the final.

"I really enjoyed the season," said Navratilova after the victory. "The pressure is there, but it's enjoyable. It's fun being part of a team."

***

In 1992, the 12th consecutive season of the league, there was a branding change: the league became known as World TeamTennis, with new franchises given to Phoenix, Tampa Bay, and Vail. As King wrote in her opening letter to fans: "Welcome to World TeamTennis. We hope you share our excitement in seeing such legends as Jimmy Connors and Martina Navratilova compete in our 11-team league for more prize money than ever."

She proclaimed that with attendance up the last season and three new franchises, the league also saw the inclusion of "more world class players to our team rosters." King wrote: "We continue to add more world class players to our team rosters. This year you'll see teenage sensation Chanda Rubin, the former champion doubles team of Scott Davis and David Pate, and Lori McNeil, who has beaten virtually all the top players on the women's tour."

Over the season, the defending champions, Atlanta Thunder, started strong by winning four straight matches. But they took on the Capitals and suffered their worst defeat ever, losing 30-14. That, however, seemingly caused them to regroup by giving them a huge wake-up call. Mark Shapiro wrote in the league's official magazine that they didn't lose a match for the rest of the year after.

"They closed the regular season with nine straight wins and easily won the Eastern Division regular season title with a 13-1 record," he wrote. "Atlanta also captured the #1 ranking in women's singles (Navratilova), men's doubles (Evernden/Steven) and mixed doubles (Evernden/Navratilova)."

In the playoffs, Newport Beach advanced to the championship match by beating Sacramento by 28-19 in the Western Divisional Semifinals. In the finals, it took out Vail by 25-23. Meanwhile, Atlanta defeated Tampa Bay by 30-22 in the Eastern Divisional Finals.

In the final, Atlanta claimed victory by beating Newport 30-17. The win broke the record for the largest victory margin in the finals. "By winning last year's title, Atlanta became the fifth team to win two championships in the history of WTT and only the third team to win back to back titles," wrote Shapiro.

"Someone always rose to the occasion and answered the call," said Navratilova at the season's conclusion. "We just practiced until we got it right."

***

In 1993, there were a record 12 teams competing for a shot at the victory and for the chance to halt the Atlanta Thunder's dominance over the last two years, and new franchises began in Florida, Minneapolis, and Kansas City. Meanwhile, top talent signed up for the league, including Tracy Austin, Bjorn Borg, and Mats Wilander. Moreover, Martina Navratilova and Jimmy Connors continued their play in the league.

And the talent continued to run deep, noted Billie Jean King. "Each year we continue to add more world-class players to our team rosters. This summer you'll see rising stars Lindsay Davenport, 15-year-old Iva Majoli, top-ranked junior Julie Steven as well as top 50 women's players Patty Fenwick and Lori McNeil," she wrote.

"Joining Connors on the men's side will be newcomers Borg and Wilander, American Jimmy Arias and two-time Australian Open champion Johan Kriek. Doubles specialist Paul Annacone, [who was ranked as high as No.3 in doubles and won the Australian Open doubles tournament in 1985], and former Wimbledon doubles winner Ken Flach will also compete in their first season of WTT," she proclaimed.

The season also saw the start to a now cherished tradition for the league: the first ever Smash Hits event to benefit the Elton John Aids Foundation, an event which was Ilana Kloss' creation. Meanwhile, the recreational league saw 340,000 players take part in the format, which was up from 165,000 in 1990.

In the West, meanwhile, Newport Beach went through the season undefeated until their final match.

Katrina Adams, Rikard Bergh, Manon Bollegraf, and Trevor Kronemann wanted to avenge their loss to the Thunder from last season. But Kansas City ended their run by taking them out 29-16 in the season's last match to make them finish 13-1, which tied records by San Antonio in 1986 and Atlanta in the last season in 1992.

"Playoff time had arrived and Wichita opened the playoffs by ousting Kansas City, 26-22, in the East Semifinal while Phoenix surprised Sacramento 24-21," according to Mike Shapiro in an overview. "That left Wichita vs. Atlanta and Newport Beach vs. Phoenix in the Divisional Finals. Those matches and the title match took place at the inaugural WTT Championship Weekend, in Atlanta, Georgia, August 6-8."

The weekend began with Wichita defeating the two-time defending champion 25-18 in the first match. It was a tight one until McNeil beat Navratilova 6-1. "I returned very well and won a lot of key points," said McNeil about the win. With the victory, there would be no three-peat, which would have been a first for the league.

"Lori was on tonight," said Navratilova. "She won the deuce games and that was the difference."

In the match between Phoenix and Newport, meanwhile, Rikard Bergh wouldn't relent to Jimmy Connors. Although he had lost twice to Connors in the regular season, he came back from 3-5 down to win the fourth set 6-5. That allowed the Dukes to grab a lead, and they never looked back. "I was long overdue," said Bergh. "I lost to him four times. I just wanted to stay out there for as long as I could and I got luck breaking back when Jimmy was serving for the set."

"He zoned for a set," said Connors. "I played matches in the finals of Wimbledon when a guy did that to me. What can you do? He played well and won."

"Winning the title was on the mind of both teams on Sunday, August 8," according to Shapiro. "Newport Beach was back for their second year in a row while Wichita was making their first appearance. A full house awaited both." The championship pitted the team with a 14-1 record against the partisan crowd.

The match ultimately came down to the very last set with Newport Beach up 21-20. "Mixed doubles was Newport Beach's strongest set, but not today, as Wichita's T.J. Middleton took over the match," wrote Shapiro. "Everything Middleton swung at went for a winner and his serve couldn't be touched."

In the end, McNeil defeated Bollegraf to give them a 26-23 victory from behind. The win marked a huge turnaround for Wichita, which finished the 1992 season 2-12.

"You really have to hand it to T.J.," said Greg Patton, Newport's coach. "He played a great aggressive doubles set. We now know what it's like running into 'Rambo.'"

"I always thought from day one we would have a winner," said Wichita's coach, Melvyn Webster. "Sometimes you have to have a little luck along the way and we were fortunate to have that."

***

The 1994 season saw even greater heights achieved by the league in its 14th season. Players taking part included Bjorn Borg, Jimmy Connors, Kevin Curren, Andres Gomez, Zina Garrison, Johan Kriek, Lori McNeil, and Martina Navratilova.

Overall, 48 players competed for $720,000 in prize money. The league also saw 12 franchises playing, including new franchises awarded to Charlotte, Idaho, and St. Louis.

In the regular season, Martina Navratilova switched from playing for the Atlanta Thunder to being part of the New Jersey Stars. She helped them secure an 11-3 regular season and also claiming the East Division title.

"Martina was the catalyst to our team, but she needed her teammates just as badly as they needed her," according to Craig Kardon, the New Jersey coach. "As she comes down to the end of the wire, she needs a little extra support to keep her going, and WTT offers that."

In the West, the Newport Beach Dukes enjoyed another tremendous season with help from Zina Garrison and 1994 Female MVP and Rookie of the Year Larisa Neiland. They became the first team in WTT history to be undefeated during the regular season.

"The Dukes' 14-0 record earned them a second West Division title and toppled the previous regular season won-loss record (13-1), which they shared with Atlanta," according to Kim Couch in an article about the season.

In the Central Division, meanwhile, the San Antonio Racquets prevailed as the defending champions, and the Wichita Advantage fell out of playoff contention due to a loss to St. Louis during the last day of the regular season.

Fast forward to the semis and the Sneakers defeated the Newport Beach team despite their undefeated play during the regular season. In fact, the Sneakers ousted them 25-16. In the other semifinal, New Jersey edged out a 28-25 win against San Antonio thanks to Navratilova's play.

In the final, Navratilova and her teammates John-Laffnie de Jager, Mariaan de Swardt, and Brian Devening claimed the title and New Jersey's first by beating the Idaho Sneakers 28-25.

This was also Navratilova's fourth WTT final. "This was sweet and we had a great team," she said. "Winning a championship is always a very emotional experience. When you get older they're that much sweeter because you know you don't have that many left."

"There were more swings in this match than Tarzan, Cheetah, and Jane. It was incredible," said Greg Patton of the Idaho Sneakers after his team lost. "Martina's experience was the difference."

***

For the league's 15th season in 1995, 10 teams competed in the league after franchises bowed out. A new team joined the league, however, in Schenectady, New York. Players competing included Zina Garrison, Martina Navratilova, Amy Frazier, and Luke and Murphy Jensen. Other newcomers included Brenda Schultz, Bryan Shelton, and Sabine Hack. The 40 players in the league that season competed to win $600,000 in prize money.

In the West semifinals, two-time champions Atlanta played the Idaho Sneakers, last year's finalists. Meanwhile, for the East, the New Jersey Stars, the defending champions and which had Navratilova on board, played the new New York OTBzz. In that match, the Stars defeated the New York team by 28-19.

In the other semi, Atlanta Thunder took out the Sneakers despite the team from Idaho winning three of the five sets played. Overall, Atlanta was more dominant in women's and mixed doubles to win 27-21.

In the championship match played in Charlotte, North Carolina, and aired on ESPN2, "The Thunder looked tough in the first half as they won the first set and forced New Jersey to tiebreakers in the other two sets," according to a league match write-up. "It was after the half that the Stars put on a show for the crowd. Navratilova defeated Zina Garrison 6-0 in women's singles."

New Jersey won the 1995 title and Martina Navratilova headlined play. Pictured (l. to r.): WTT co-founder Billie Jean King, Brad Pearce, Martina Navratilova, Richard Matuszewski, Mariaan de Swardt, Coach Craig Kardon, and team GM Becky Vuksta. Photo: World TeamTennis

Garrison, meanwhile, struggled with heat illness. "I just didn't play well," she said. "I got behind and then it just started to steamroll."

But Atlanta wasn't to be defeated that easily. They tried to come back in the last set. "The Thunder tied the set at 4-4 and had game point at 4-5 with the chance to take the match to its third tiebreaker. However, Katrina Adams and Garrison lost to Mariaan de Swardt and Navratilova 6-4."

That cemented the win for New Jersey's victory 28-20 to claim their back-to-back titles and capped off the 15th anniversary of the league. "Martina played well. She really lifted the level of her game," said New Jersey's coach Craig Kardon after the win.

WTT FINALS **1991**

Atlanta Thunder

Los Angeles Strings

WTT FINALS **1992**

Atlanta Thunder

Newport Beach Dukes

WTT FINALS **1993**

Wichita Advantage

Newport Beach Dukes

WTT FINALS 1994

New Jersey Stars   28

Idaho Sneakers   25

WTT FINALS 1995

New Jersey Stars   28

Atlanta Thunder   20

Chapter Five: Seasons Twenty-One to Twenty-Five (1996-2000):

Sacramento Success

1996 TEAMS & PLAYERS:

Atlanta Thunder:	Luke Jensen, Murphy Jensen, Rebecca Jensen, Lindsay Lee, Olivier Morel, Patricia Tarabini. COACH: Brian Devilliers
Delaware Smash:	Nicole Arendt, John-Laffnie de Jager, Kelly Jones, Martina Navratilova, Pam Shriver, Tami Whitlinger-Jones. COACH: Charlton Eagle, Assistant COACH: Billie Jean King
Idaho Sneakers:	Jane Chi, Amy Frazier, Brett Hansen-Dent, Jon Leach. COACH: Greg Patton
Kansas City Explorers:	Mariaan de Swardt, Doug Flach, Ken Flach, Bret Garnett, Debbie Graham, John McEnroe, Lori McNeil. COACH: Paul Smith
New York OTBzz:	Patricia Hy-Boulais, Kristine Radford, Dave Randall, Arantxa Sanchez-Vicario, Kenny Thorne. COACH: Inderjit Singh
Sacramento Capitals:	Brian MacPhie, Rachel McQuillan, Sandon Stolle, Caroline Vis. Player/ COACH: Scott Davis
St. Louis Aces:	Sandra Cacic, Michael Joyce, Rick Leach, Lisa Raymond, Rennae Stubbs. COACH: Rick Flach
Springfield Lasers:	Zina Garrison-Jackson, Trevor Kronemann, David MacPherson, Kathy Rinaldi-Stunkel, Marianne Werdel-Witmeyer. COACH: Mervyn Webster
WTT FINALS *(in Wesley Chapel, Fla.):*	St. Louis Aces def. Delaware Smash 27-16

1997 TEAMS & PLAYERS:

Delaware Smash:	Nicole Arendt, Patricia Hy(-Boulais), Luke Jensen, Murphy Jensen, Lori McNeil. COACH: Charlton Eagle
Idaho Sneakers:	Katrina Adams, Amy Frazier, Ginger Helgeson-Nielsen, Sargis Sargisian, Bryan Shelton. COACH: Greg Patton
Kansas City Explorers:	John-Laffnie de Jager, Mary Joe Fernandez, Ann Grossman, Patricia Tarabini, Caroline Vis, Wesley Whitehouse. COACH: Paul Smith

Milwaukee Racqueteers:	Tami Whitlinger-Jones, Christo van Rensburg, Jack Waite, Linda Wild. COACH: Rick Vetter
New York OTBzz:	Mariaan de Swardt, Debbie Graham, Joannette Kruger, Angela Lettiere, Dave Randall, Brenda Schultz-McCarthy, Kenny Thorne, Tim Triguiero. COACH: Inderjit Singh
Sacramento Capitals:	Lindsay Davenport, Ellis Ferreira, Chris Gerety, Kristine Kunce, Mirjana Lucic, Brian MacPhie, Corina Morariu, Richey Reneberg, Player/COACH: Scott Davis
St. Louis Aces:	Michael Hill, Robbie Koenig, Rick Leach, Maja Muric, Lisa Raymond, Brie Rippner, Rennae Stubbs. COACH: Jack Levitt
Springfield Lasers:	Trevor Kronemann, David MacPherson, Larisa Neiland, Kathy Rinaldi-Stunkel. COACH: Mervyn Webster
WTT FINALS *(in Orlando, Fla.)*:	Sacramento Capitals won title due to regular season standings (Finals rained out)

1998 TEAMS & PLAYERS:

Delaware Smash:	Elena Bovina, Dawn Buth, Luke Jensen, Murphy Jensen, Lori McNeil, Martina Navratilova. COACH: Mike DePalmer, Sr.
Idaho Sneakers:	Gigi Fernandez, Neville Godwin, Debbie Graham, Mark Keil, Patrick McEnroe, Jared Palmer, Katie Schlukebir, Wesley Whitehouse. COACH: Michael Robertson
Kansas City Explorers:	Jimmy Connors, Mariaan de Swardt, John-Laffnie de Jager, Robbie Koenig, Patricia Tarabini, Caroline Vis. COACH: Paul Smith
New York OTBzz:	Mary Joe Fernandez, Geoff Grant, Liezel Horn, Rachel McQuillan, Nana Miyagi, Louise Pleming, Dave Randall. COACH: Inderjit Singh
Sacramento Capitals:	Lindsay Davenport, Kristine Kunce, Fang Li, Brian MacPhie, Corina Morariu, Richey Reneberg, Brie Rippner, Sandon Stolle. COACH: Scott Davis
St. Louis Aces:	Ginger Helgeson-Nielson, Michael Hill, Rick Leach, Tara Snyder. COACH: Aleco Preovolos
Springfield Lasers:	Katrina Adams, Brent Haygarth, David MacPherson, T.J. Middleton, Larisa Neiland. COACH: Trevor Kronemann
WTT FINALS *(in Sacramento, Calif.)*:	Sacramento Capitals def. New York OTBzz 30-13

1999 TEAMS & PLAYERS:

Delaware Smash:	Mary Joe Fernandez, Jim Grabb, Patrick McEnroe, Lori McNeil, Lilia Osterloh, Mike Sell. COACH: Brad Dancer
Idaho Sneakers:	Bob Bryan, Mike Bryan, Jane Chi, Mirjana Lucic, Brie Rippner, Katie Schlukebir. COACH: Wayne Bryan
Kansas City Explorers:	John-Laffnie de Jager, Mariaan de Swardt, Oliver Freelove, Liezel Horn, Alistair Hunt, Monica Seles. COACH: Paul Smith
Sacramento Capitals:	Elena Likhovtseva, Brian MacPhie, Kimberly Po, Richey Reneberg, Chanda Rubin, Jessica Steck. COACH: Scott Davis
St. Louis Aces:	Debbie Graham, Brent Haygarth, Murphy Jensen, Stefan Kruger, Tara Snyder. COACH: Mike DePalmer, Sr.
Schenectady County Electrics:	Geoff Grant, T.J. Middleton, Martina Navratilova, Louise Pleming, Samantha Smith. COACH: Gerry Cuva
Springfield Lasers:	David MacPherson, Larisa Neiland, Grant Stafford, Elena Tatarkova. COACH: Ken Goodall
WTT FINALS *(in Sacramento, Calif.)*:	Sacramento Capitals def. Springfield Lasers 23-15

2000 TEAMS & PLAYERS:
EASTERN CONFERENCE:

Delaware Smash:	Mariaan de Swardt, Mary Joe Fernandez, Geoff Grant, Lori McNeil, Mike Sell, Serena Williams. COACH: Brad Dancer
Hartford FoxForce:	James Blake, Doug Bohaboy, Liezel Horn, Murphy Jensen, Bethanie Mattek, Monica Seles. COACH: Paul Assaiante
New York Hamptons:	Jim Courier, Erika De Lone, Tina Krizan, Patrick McEnroe, Jonathan Stark, Eric Taino, Monique Viele. COACH: Dickie Herbst
Schenectady County Electrics:	Nannie de Villiers, Brent Haygarth, Michael Hill, Martina Navratilova, Mary Pierce, Nicole Pratt, Jolene Watanabe. COACH: Gerry Cuva

WESTERN CONFERENCE:

Idaho Sneakers:	Jane Chi, Kim Grant, Levar Harper-Griffith, Andy Roddick, Katie Schlukebir. COACH: Jim Moortgat
Kansas City Explorers:	Jeff Coetzee, Jennifer Hopkins, Alistair Hunt, Holly Parkinson. COACH: Paul Smith
Sacramento Capitals:	Elena Likhovtseva, Brian MacPhie, Richey Reneberg, Brie Rippner. COACH: Kevin Forbes
St. Louis Aces:	Jason Cook, Surina de Beer, Luke Jensen, Michael Joyce, Nana Miyagi, Venus Williams. COACH: Kyle Mayberry
Springfield Lasers:	Dawn Buth, Debbie Graham, Lina Krasnoroutskaya, David MacPherson, Larisa Neiland, Grant Stafford, Tara Snyder. COACH: Ken Goodall
WTT FINALS *(in Flushing Meadows, N.Y.)*:	Sacramento Capitals def. Delaware Smash 21-20

The 15th anniversary finished with a bang to cap off the early '90s. The past five years were differentiated by the powerful performances of Martina Navratilova, as well as the continued leadership of Billie Jean King and Ilana Kloss, and the slate of seasons to head into the new century signified the dominance of the Sacramento Capitals.

Additionally, WTT captured new talent in singles, doubles and mixed doubles, including John McEnroe, one of the best American men's tennis player to ever pick up a racquet in the Open Era. He also proved to be an ardent WTT player and supporter throughout and after his career.

In 1996, the 16th consecutive season of WTT featured the inclusion of McEnroe, while Navratilova joined once again as well as Arantxa Sanchez Vicario, who was ranked the No. 3 player in the world to finish 1995. There was also a change in the schedule thanks to the Summer Olympics being played that year.

"I really like our lineup this year," said King. "I think the move to September enabled us to get some players we wouldn't have otherwise."

She added: "And, it's always great starting your season right after a Grand Slam tournament. For us, particularly in this country, it's great starting right after the US Open."

"While WTT dropped two teams from last year, Ilana Kloss, WTT Executive Director, feels the eight teams going to the post this season are all solid franchises," according to the season's official magazine.

"I'm very pleased with the team ownership," said Kloss ahead of the season's start. "Every owner we have now is a real tennis person and they've done a great job."

"You're only as strong as your front office and that's been a major league concern all along," she added, "but we feel very good about that this year."

King predicted what the season would look like given the influx of talent. "It's a real wide open race," she said. "It looks like any team could win it if they play well together." Over 100,000 people would end up watching WTT matches over the course of the season.

The eight seasons that played in the league in 1996 were the Atlanta Thunder, Delaware Smash, Idaho Sneakers, Kansas City Explorers, New York OTBzz, Sacramento Capitals, St. Louis Aces, and the Springfield Lasers.

The final four of the season produced a match between the Delaware Smash and Sacramento Capitals for the Championship Weekend, which was held at Saddlebrook Resort in Wesley Chapel, Florida. "With a last minute replacement of Cyril Suk for Sandon Stolle, the Capitals went down in men's doubles to the highly rated team of de Jager and Jones to open the match," according to the league's match notes.

"Brian MacPhie then returned the favor in men's singles when he beat Jones 6-3. Leading 15-12 at the half, the Smash were optimistic with their strongest events yet to come," it continued. "A surprise victory by Rachel McQuillan over Navratilova in women's singles put the pressure on Delaware in the final set. Navratilova teamed with Nicole Arendt, however, to seal the match in women's doubles, giving the team from Delaware a 25-21 victory.

In the other match, St. Louis grabbed momentum early by winning women's doubles and singles. Lisa Raymond, who finished as the WTT Female Rookie of the Year and Female MVP, was also number one in women's singles, doubles, and mixed doubles. She propelled the team to a decisive 28-18 win over two-time champions, the Atlanta Thunder.

Although Raymond was far and away the best women's player over the season, she ironically was the only player to lose a set in the championship round against the Smash. "WTT veteran Martina Navratilova applied constant pressure by rushing the net on Raymond and claimed a decisive 6-3 win in women's singles," according to the match report. "The Aces rebounded with a 6-1 dismissal of the Smash in men's doubles to give St. Louis a five-game halftime advantage."

The Aces' Michael Joyce upped his level to claim men's doubles and singles. "Our doubles was a big momentum change," he said after the win. "That definitely took the pressure off for the remainder of the match."

The St. Louis Aces defeated the Delaware Smash in 1996 to become the league champions. Pictured (l. to r.): Coach Rick Flach, Michael Joyce, Rick Leach, Lisa Raymond and Rennae Stubbs. Photo: World TeamTennis

The Aces dominated the second half of the match, too. "Rennae Stubbs and Rick Leach, the WTT #1 ranked mixed doubles tandem, scored a 6-3 victory over the highly touted pair of Navratilova and John-Laffnie de Jager to seal the match."

The Aces won 27-16 for the title. "We were the number one team all season," said Raymond after the victory. "We had to do it in the big match and today was the big match."

***

The 1997 season also featured a slate of teams from across the U.S. in action, along with a new team in Milwaukee. Marquee players to join the league included Lindsay Davenport, Mary Joe Fernandez, Amy Frazier, Larisa Neiland, the Jensen brothers, and Richey Reneberg.

The season was a historic one in that Championship Weekend. But not for the best reasons. Held at Disney's Wide World of Sports Complex in Orlando, Florida, in conjunction with the recreational league finals, the event was totally rained out with seven days and seven nights of rain ("We never saw blue skies until the players had to leave," according to King). Therefore, the team's champion to receive the first annual King Trophy, named after Billie Jean King and Larry King, was decided not by a match but rather by the regular season.

The eight teams that played in the 1997 Professional League were the Delaware Smash, Idaho Sneakers, Kansas City Explorers, Milwaukee Racqueteers, New York OTBzz, Sacramento Capitals, St. Louis Aces, and the Springfield Lasers. With an impressive 13-1 record, the Sacramento Capitals claimed the title thanks to "El Nino" raining out any play during the weekend.

Lindsay Davenport was behind the team's victory in the regular season thanks to her success during the team's 14 matches over the summer. "Playing in her second WTT season, [she] led the Sacramento Capitals to their first-ever WTT title," according to an article in the league's Supertiebreaker magazine. "With a .629 winning percentage in women's singles, a .622 winning percentage in women's doubles (with Kristine Kunce) and a .579 winning percentage in mixed doubles (with Scott Davis, Ellis Ferreira and Brian MacPhie), Davenport secured first place in each event she played. In addition to being named WTT Female Rookie of the Year in 1993, the world's second-ranked women's tennis player grabbed the WTT Female Most Valuable Player of the Year award in 1997."

"The key thing about this team is that we all got along," said Capitals coach Scott David in an interview. "In World TeamTennis, chemistry is critical and that helped a great deal to mesh our team, both on and off court."

In summing up the season, league stories noted that "although 'El Nino' prohibited any play at Championship Weekend, the 1997 WTT regular season did not lack excitement."

Overall, the teams attracted more than 100,000 fans during the year.

***

Following the unorthodox end to the last season, 1998 began with earnest as the league secured a new partnership with DuPont as the title sponsor of both the professional and recreational leagues. WTT also made a big change to switch things up: it split the pro league's season into two parts, with the first half played from July 8 to 26 and the second half played from September 12 to 20. The Championship Weekend was scheduled for September 23 to 26.

Among the top players to take part in the league were Lindsay Davenport (last season's powerhouse), Mary Joe Fernandez, and the return of both Jimmy Connors and Martina Navratilova.

In 1998, the Sacramento Capitals defeated the New York OTBzz by a score of 30-13 to win their second of six WTT titles. Pictured (l. to r.): Kristine Kunce, owner Jayna Osborne, owner Ramey Osborne, Richey Reneberg, Brian MacPhie, Scott Davis, Lindsay Davenport, Corina Morariu and WTT co-founder Billie Jean King. Photo: World TeamTennis

In addition, the WTT Junior Program merged with the USTA Jr. TeamTennis Program to help spread the WTT format to even more young players across the nation with a passion for the sport.

In the semis, the Sacramento Capitals, the defending champions, headed to the final with a 29-20 win in Overtime over the Springfield Lasers. They were looking for redemption after rain forced them to take the title without playing a point during the Championship Weekend. Meanwhile, the New York OTBzz advanced to the final with a 28-18 victory over the St. Louis Aces.

"The match began with the Capitals' Brian MacPhie and Richey Reneberg upsetting the DuPont WTT first ranked tandem of Geoff Grant and Dave Randall in men's doubles," according to an the official match report. "Lindsay Davenport next routed New York's Rachel McQuillan 6-1 to keep the momentum going."

In the next set, the combination of Davenport and MacPhie was too strong for the duo of Nana Miyagi and Dave Randall. The Americans won 6-3 to snatch a ten-game lead going into halftime against the team from New York.

"Reneberg, the 1997 Male Rookie of the Year, dominated in men's singles with a 6-1 win over Grant, who was named the 1998 DuPont WTT Male Rookie of the Year," the article continued. "Davenport and Corina Morariu then sealed the match with a 6-4 upset of McQuillan and Miyagi in women's doubles."

The victory and the King Trophy was awarded to the Capitals for the second straight year—but this was the first time it was due to their exceptional play in the championship match, after their first was rained out. The win was also one of the most dominant in league history, as the Capitals defeated the New York OTBzz by 30-13.

"Sacramento deserved to win the title today," said Kloss after the match. "They really rose to the occasion and proved what teamwork can do."

***

For the 1999 season, the league decided to change a key element of each match: sets were shortened from six games to win to just five. Once again, the league kept the season split into two, with the first half in the summer and the later taking place in September. There were seven teams playing total.

Veteran players to take part in the league included Navratilova, the Jensen brothers and Mary Joe Fernandez. It also welcomed new players to the fold, including Monica Seles and Bob and Mike Bryan, two up-and-coming doubles players, and identical twins.

Navratilova took the season to meditate on the meaning of teamwork in an article for the league's official magazine. "Yes, the ultimate confrontation, at least in singles, is a most wonderful one-on-one situation," she began. "However, to get there and be successful, requires a team effort, from the moms and dads who have been driving their 'prodigy' to their appointed lessons, to the psychologist who makes sure the 'star' is in the perfect frame of mind, to all the people in between, it is a team effort."

Navratilova said team tennis was a "natural progression" for her thanks to growing up in the Czech Republic playing and training with teammates.

"There are so many aspects of World TeamTennis that really appeal to me," she continued. "First and foremost is the fact that women and men can participate and contribute equally."

"But what I thrive on is getting into the nitty gritty and the ability to give and get feedback during the match," according to Navratilova. "Sitting on the bench, I enjoy talking to the coach and players—what isn't working and why, what should we tell the players on the change of ends or even yell during the set." In singles, meanwhile, she said she enjoyed the ability to get encouragement from her teammates.

"Like I said, tennis is a team sport and I like being a team player," she added. "Or maybe, as Craig Kardon, the 1992 WTT Coach of the Year and my personal coach from 1989 until retirement, used to tell me—I just like to tell people what to do."

In the professional league play, the finals were set between the Sacramento Capitals gunning for a record third-straight WTT title versus the Springfield Lasers. "The Capitals had won two straight titles," a match report says. "But the Lasers weren't intimidated for a minute. Doubles veteran Larisa Neiland, partnered with Elena Tatarkova, proved why they were the league's best doubles team with a crisp 5-3 win over Likhovtseva and Jessica Steck."

The Capitals' Likhovtseva wasn't discouraged by the loss, however. "Armed with penetrating groundstrokes on both sides, she summarily whipped Tatarkova, 5-1," the report continued. "Then she promptly joined forces with her mixed doubles partner, lefty bomber, Brian MacPhie, to down Neiland and David Macpherson, 5-2, giving the Capitals a commanding 13-8 halftime lead."

"Elena came through in a big way," said Kloss at the time. "Her team was counting on her and even after that opening loss, she rebounded and completely reversed the momentum."

Richey Reneberg next took out Macpherson 5-3 to get the team even closer to the three-peat. "Reneberg and MacPhie squeaked out a 5-4 (5-3) win over Macpherson and Rick Leach, sealing a 23-15 victory," the article notes.

"We're talking dynasty," said Kloss. "What Sacramento's been able to accomplish is incredible."

"I think what we've seen is that there's a great combination of inspired tennis and wonderful community involvement," she continued about the historic win and the first-ever time a team had won three straight WTT titles. "The atmosphere that's been created is a big part of what's made the players so successful."

***

With the Sacramento Capitals the winningest team in WTT history, the new millennium started with a bang and with nine teams competing for a chance at the King Trophy. Eight of them, of course, wanted to unseat the Capitals from their dominance over the league.

The year 2000 also marked the 20th consecutive season of the league and nine teams looking to compete to win, which was up from just seven the year prior.

"Heading into the 21st century, WTT is eagerly kicking off one of its most exciting season," according to the official magazine. "Now celebrating its 20th consecutive season, WTT is taking big steps."

Two new franchises joined for the year: the Hartford FoxForce and New York Hamptons, which was owned by Patrick McEnroe, brother to John.

"Playing WTT the last couple of years, I was amazed at how much I enjoyed it," said Patrick McEnroe. "I really loved playing college tennis at Stanford and representing the U.S. in Davis Cup, so here was another great forum for that team concept."

"Becoming part of WTT is also a wonderful way to get involved in the New York community. They played such a big role in helping me become a player," he said.

***

Highlight #5: Welcoming the Williams Sisters

The season marked the start of something momentous for the league as well as for tennis: the Williams sisters joined just as their careers began surging to success.

Serena, who won the US Open the year before to become the first African-American woman since Althea Gibson to win a major title, played for the Delaware Smash, and Venus joined the St. Louis Aces.

"Venus and Serena Williams are revolutionizing tennis," said Billie Jean King at the time. "They're bringing in all sorts of people to tennis. Their big-time, aggressive games make them wonderful to watch."

"They've got the goods," said King.

Venus has expressed optimism for her experience with the league in the past and for its future. "It was so exciting for us. My first World TeamTennis match was in sometime around 1990 when I was 10 years old," she said in an interview with WTT's web site.

Over the years, the sisters have collected a total of six WTT titles. Serena's first team was with the Delaware Smash in 2000, followed by the St. Louis Aces in 2007 and the Washington Kastles from 2008 to 2011.

Venus Williams competed for the St. Louis Aces, the Delaware Smash, the Philadelphia Freedoms, and the Washington Kastles. Photo: CameraworkUSA

Meanwhile, Venus has played for the St. Louis Aces, the Delaware Smash, the Philadelphia Freedoms, and the Washington Kastles, for which she's helped claim three titles. In 2012, the elder sister was named the Finals MVP.

"My first experience was even in the 80s, so I feel like I've done a good 25 years with World TeamTennis," said Venus in an interview. "I'm looking forward to going for that 50th anniversary as well."

***

Joining the sisters were a slate of other top players, including up-and-coming Americans Andy Roddick and James Blake, Jim Courier, Monica Seles, and WTT veteran Martina Navratilova. They were joined by McEnroe, Mary Pierce, Mary Joe Fernandez, and Mariaan de Swardt."

In the professional league, the Sacramento Capitals were bidding to win four straight titles. The season's championship match took place at the home of the US Open, and for the fourth time in as many years the Capitals secured victory and even more WTT history.

In the final, the team played the Delaware Smash.

"What a way to close out [the] season," said the official match report. "The Grandstand Court was rocking, the championship match was tied at 16-16 going into the final set, when three-time League MVP Brian MacPhie and partner Elena Likhovtseva surged ahead of Geoff Grand and 2000 MVP Mariaan de Swardt of the Smash, for the win."

Along with claiming four straight titles, the Capitals made even more history in pro sports: They became the first team since the NHL's New York Islanders to win a league championship in four straight seasons.

"Nowhere else in sports do you see both genders and such a diversity of generations, playing styles and nationalities working together," said King about the players and the league. "The mentoring that goes on helps make everyone a better player and in the process, fans see even more competitive dramatic matches."

"You see players improve very rapidly during the season, and this in turn helps them do even better in tournaments," she said.

WTT FINALS **1996**

| St. Louis Aces | 27 |
| Delaware Smash | 16 |

WTT FINALS **1997**

Sacramento Capitals
won title due to regular season standings
(finals rained out)

WTT FINALS 1998

Sacramento Capitals — 30

New York OTBzz — 13

WTT FINALS 1999

Sacramento Capitals — 23

Springfield Lasers — 15

WTT FINALS 2000

Sacramento Capitals — 21

Delaware Smash — 20

Chapter Six: Seasons Twenty-Six to Thirty (2001-2005):

A New Era

2001 TEAMS & PLAYERS:
EASTERN CONFERENCE:

Delaware Smash:	John-Laffnie de Jager, Mariaan de Swardt, Martina Navratilova, Holly Parkinson, Mike Sell. COACH: Brad Dancer
Hartford FoxForce:	Luke Jensen, Murphy Jensen, Sonya Jeyaseelan, Mirjana Lucic, Magdalena Maleeva, Monica Seles. COACH: Paul Assaiante
New York Buzz:	Mahesh Bhupathi, Justin Bower, Jonathan Chu, Jill Craybas, Nannie de Villiers. COACH: Eric Kutner
New York Hamptons:	Jan-Michael Gambill, Tina Krizan, John McEnroe, Patrick McEnroe, Katarina Srebotnik, Jonathan Stark. COACH: Dickie Herbst
Philadelphia Freedoms:	Jimmy Connors, David Di Lucia, Don Johnson, Lisa Raymond, Rennae Stubbs. COACH: Raja Chaudhuri

WESTERN CONFERENCE:

Kansas City Explorers:	Jeff Coetzee, Brent Haygarth, Michael Lang, Tara Snyder, Jessica Steck. COACH: Paul Smith.
Sacramento Capitals:	Kim Adamson, Dawn Buth, Maureen Drake, Mark Knowles, Elena Likhovtseva, Tatiana Panova, Brian MacPhie. COACH: Kevin Forbes
St. Louis Aces:	Manon Bollegraf, Allison Bradshaw, Lindsay Davenport, Rick Leach, Jared Palmer, Andy Roddick. COACH: Kevin Epley
Springfield Lasers:	David MacPherson, Anastasia Myskina, Katie Schlukebir, David Wheaton. COACH: Trevor Kronemann
WTT FINALS (in Flushing Meadows, N.Y.):	Philadelphia Freedoms def. Springfield Lasers 20-18

2002 TEAMS & PLAYERS:
EASTERN CONFERENCE:

Delaware Smash:	Tracey Almeda-Singian, Paul Goldstein, Brent Haygarth, Scott Humphries, Jana Novotna, Samantha Reeves, Maria Sharapova, Jolene Watanabe. COACH: Craig Kardon

Hartford FoxForce:	Cam Bhuta, James Blake, Geoff Grant, Luke Jensen, Murphy Jensen, Rossana Neffa-de los Rios, Meghann Shaughnessy, Bryanne Stewart. COACH: Paul Assaiante
New York Buzz:	Mahesh Bhupathi, Justin Bower, Lindsay Davenport, Nannie de Villiers, Liezel Huber. COACH: Eric Kutner
New York Hamptons:	Robert Kendrick, Tina Krizan, John McEnroe, Katarina Srebotnik, Player/COACH: Patrick McEnroe
Philadelphia Freedoms:	Corina Morariu, Mark Philippoussis, Todd Reid, Jonathan Stark, Jessica Steck, Alexandra Stevenson. COACH: Mike DePalmer, Jr.

WESTERN CONFERENCE:

Kansas City Explorers:	Laura Granville, Rick Leach, Rachel McQuillan, Max Mirnyi, Michael Tebbutt. COACH: Paul Smith
Sacramento Capitals:	Andre Agassi, Ashley Harkleroad, Mark Knowles, Elena Likhovtseva, Brian MacPhie, Brie Rippner, Dimitry Tursunov. COACH: Wayne Bryan
St. Louis Aces:	Olga Barabanschikova, Amanda Coetzer, Andrew Florent, Holly Parkinson, Andy Roddick, Dusan Vemic. COACH: Aleco Preovolos
Springfield Lasers:	David MacPherson, Anastasia Myskina, Katie Schlukebir, David Wheaton. COACH: Trevor Kronemann
WTT FINALS *(in Flushing Meadows, N.Y.):*	Sacramento Capitals def. New York Buzz 21-13

2003 TEAMS & PLAYERS:
EASTERN CONFERENCE:

Delaware Smash:	Paul Goldstein, Liezel Huber, Scott Humphries, Samantha Reeves. COACH: Craig Kardon
Hartford FoxForce:	James Blake, Stephen Huss, Martina Muller, Milagros Sequera, Meghann Shaughnessy, Jeff Tarango. COACH: Pete Bradshaw
New York Buzz:	Boris Becker, Justin Bower, Nannie de Villiers, Don Johnson, Shenay Perry, Shaun Rudman. COACH: Eric Kutner
New York Sportimes:	Bea Bielik, Dustin Brown, Ellis Ferreira, John Paul Fruttero, Marissa Irvin, John McEnroe, Patrick McEnroe, Shuai Peng. COACH: Joe Guliano
Philadelphia Freedoms:	Jill Craybas, Erika de Lone, Andrew Florent, Nathan Healey, Martina Navratilova, Tina Pisnik, Elena Tatarkova, Vera Zvonareva. COACH: Judy Dixon

WESTERN CONFERENCE:

Kansas City Explorers:	Laura Granville, Anniko Kapros, Anna Kournikova, Rick Leach, Rachel McQuillan, David Wheaton. COACH: Paul Smith
Newport Beach Breakers:	Lindsay Davenport, Eva Dyrberg, Josh Eagle, Brian MacPhie, Jewel Peterson, Maria Sharapova. COACH: Dick Leach

Sacramento Capitals:	Andre Agassi, Ally Baker, Mark Knowles, Daniel Nestor, Elena Likhovtseva. COACH: Wayne Bryan
St. Louis Aces:	Nicole Arendt, John-Laffnie de Jager, Amir Hadad, Andy Roddick, Brie Rippner, Julia Vakulenko. COACH: Greg Patton
Springfield Lasers:	Christina Fusano, Andrew Kratzmann, David MacPherson, Nana Miyagi, Anastasia Myskina, Rossana Neffa-de los Rios, Glenn Weiner. COACH: Trevor Kronemann
WTT FINALS *(in Flushing Meadows, N.Y.):*	Delaware Smash def. Sacramento Capitals 21-14

2004 TEAMS & PLAYERS:
EASTERN CONFERENCE:

Delaware Smash:	Paul Goldstein, Liezel Huber, Samantha Reeves, David Wheaton. COACH: Brad Dancer
Hartford FoxForce:	Mardy Fish, Don Johnson, Lisa McShea, Milagros Sequera, Meghann Shaughnessy, Wesley Whitehouse. COACH: Paul Assaiante
New York Buzz:	Justin Bower, Viktoriya Kutuzova, Martina Navratilova, Shaun Rudman, Bryanne Stewart. COACH: Jolene Watanabe
New York Sportimes:	Bea Bielik, Ruxandra Dragomir, Hermes Gamonal, Monica Seles, Joe Sirianni. COACH: John Roddick
Philadelphia Freedoms:	Josh Eagle, John Paul Fruttero, Patrick Rafter, Lisa Raymond, Elena Tatarkova. COACH: Craig Kardon

WESTERN CONFERENCE:

Kansas City Explorers:	Alex Kim, Anna Kournikova, David Macpherson, Rachel McQuillan, Silvija Talaja. COACH: Paul Smith
Newport Beach Breakers:	Bob Bryan, Mike Bryan, Ramon Delgado, Ellis Ferreira, Aniko Kapros, Nana Miyagi, Maria Sharapova. COACH: Dick Leach
Sacramento Capitals:	Andre Agassi, Mark Knowles, Anastassia Rodionova, Dmitry Tursunov, Nicole Vaidisova. COACH: Wayne Bryan
St. Louis Aces:	Robby Ginepri, Amir Hadad, Kelly McCain, Tzipora Obziler, Brian Wilson. COACH: Greg Patton
Springfield Lasers:	Daja Bedanova, Jalal Chafai, Andrew Kratzmann, Kristen Schlukebir. COACH: Trevor Kronemann
WTT FINALS *(in Flushing Meadows, N.Y.):*	Newport Beach Breakers def. Delaware Smash 23-17

2005 TEAMS & PLAYERS:
EASTERN CONFERENCE:

Boston Lobsters:	Daja Bedanova, James Blake, Thomas Blake, Jonathan Chu, Johan Landsberg, Martina Navratilova, Kristen Schlukebir. COACH: Anne Smith
Delaware Smash:	Roger Anderson, Liezel Huber, Robbie Koenig, Wayne Odesnik, Chanelle Scheepers, Rennae Stubbs, Venus Williams. COACH: Mariaan De Swardt
Hartford FoxForce:	Don Johnson, Lisa McShea, Mark Philippoussis, Milagros Sequera, Meghann Shaughnessy, Wesley Whitehouse. COACH: Aleco Prevolos
New York Buzz:	Jim Courier, Jaymon Crabb, Evie Dominikovic, Bryanne Stewart, Brian Vahaly. COACH: Jolene Watanabe
New York Sportimes:	Natalie Grandin, Martina Hingis, Jenny Hopkins, Robert Kendrick, John McEnroe, Mark Merklein. COACH: Joe Guiliano
Philadelphia Freedoms:	Josh Eagle, John Paul Fruttero, Carly Gullickson, Patrick Rafter, Lisa Raymond, Elena Tatarkova. COACH: Craig Kardon

WESTERN CONFERENCE:

Houston Wranglers:	Ansley Cargill, Mardy Fish, Ashley Fisher, Edina Gallovits, Steffi Graf, Ryan Newport. COACH: John Lucas
Kansas City Explorers:	Bob Bryan, Mike Bryan, Laura Granville, David Macpherson, Brian MacPhie, Nana Miyagi, Samantha Reeves. COACH: Paul Smith
Newport Beach Breakers:	Katerina Bondarenko, Devin Bowen, Ramon Delgado, Anastasia Rodionova, Maria Sharapova. COACH: Dick Leach
Sacramento Capitals:	Mark Knowles, Anna Kournikova, Elena Likhovtseva, Nicole Vaidisova, Sam Warburg. COACH: Wayne Bryan
St. Louis Aces:	Jonathan Erlich, Jamea Jackson, Andy Ram, Andy Roddick, Jennifer Russell. COACH: Greg Patton
Springfield Lasers:	Rik De Voest, Rick Leach, Kelly McCain, Kaysie Smashey. COACH: Trevor Kronemann
WTT FINALS *(in Sacramento, Calif.):*	New York Sportimes def. Newport Beach Breakers 21-18

After the Sacramento Capitals took control over the last five seasons with a series of wins, seasons 26 to 30 saw a shifting of the guard even as they continued bidding for more titles to add to their collection. Moreover, the competition became even fiercer with players such as the Williams sisters, Anna Kournikova, Andre Agassi, and Andy Roddick.

The 2001 season, meanwhile, brought back a franchise that helped begin the league: the Philadelphia Freedoms and Billie Jean King's original team. The Freedoms, of course, inspired Elton John's song and were a welcome addition to the league, bringing the number of teams competing for the King Trophy to nine. And who better to play on the revived team than Jimmy Connors?

Other top contenders and marquee players to grace the multi-colored WTT courts that year included Davenport, Seles, Roddick, Jan-Michael Gambill, Jana Novotna, and, last but not least, John McEnroe.

The rejoining of the Freedoms caused waves for the league. "They could easily have been called the comeback kids," noted a review of the 2001 season. "In their inaugural season, the 'new' reincarnated Philadelphia Freedoms defeated the Springfield Lasers 20-18, to win the King trophy and the 2001 WTT championship title."

In doing so, no longer were the Sacramento Capitals the same unwavering contenders who had won four straight titles.

"With this victory, the Freedoms did what few pro sports expansion teams have been able to do... capture a national championship in their first season," according to match reports.

The match began with Lisa Raymond and Rennae Stubbs of the Freedoms losing—despite being the top-ranked women's doubles team—to Anastasia Myskina and Katie Schlukebir in the first set by 5-4.

But despite the slow start to the day and the championship match held at the home of the US Open, the Freedoms rallied back well. Indeed, Raymond turned around her form to win 5-1 in women's singles. In mixed doubles, she played and won yet again, beating Schlukebir and David MacPherson.

"Springfield fought back," said the match report. "David Wheaton defeated Don Johnson in men's singles; the Lasers surged ahead 16-13 going into the final set and defeated Philadelphia in men's doubles. Then the score was 19-18, Philadelphia."

The match went into Overtime, but the Freedoms halted any chance at defeat by claiming the first game to win the King Trophy in their first season back in action 20-18.

***

Highlight #6: Ilana Kloss Takes Charge as CEO

With WTT into a new millennium, there was a big change for the league from a leadership perspective, too: Ilana Kloss took over for Billie Jean King as CEO and commissioner of the league, a position that was well-deserved given her commitment to WTT from the very beginning.

"I have been involved in World TeamTennis at every level, as player, coach and now as the CEO and Commissioner of the League, and it has been a privilege to watch this unique tennis concept evolve into a success," she wrote in her letter to fans for the first time as chief executive of WTT.

"We're not only older, we're better," she added. "It has been personally gratifying to me to watch the evolution of WTT as both entertainment and a vehicle for terrific tennis."

Kloss added: and "as a place for players to revel in the pure enjoyment of team competition while hitting the fuzz off the ball!"

Ilana Kloss took over as Executive Director in 1991 and became the league CEO in 2001, succeeding Billie Jean King. Photo: World TeamTennis.

In an interview, Kloss discussed the time she first met Billie Jean King when she served as her ball girl during a tournament in South Africa. "Timing is really everything, and I think there are certain moments in time that you can mark as critical," she said.

"Flash forward six or seven years I actually was playing there," said Kloss.

She played in the league soon after, during its first season. "For me, it was really kind of making it to the big leagues, and I had always love being part of the team," Kloss said of her experience with the Golden Gaters at the Oakland Coliseum that first season.

"No question that the compensation offered was unbelievable," she said. "I mean, to be honest, the deal that, you know, they end up negotiating was more that my father earned. So, relatively speaking, you know, it was huge, and when you're starting out in the career that's really important."

Kloss said that, along with the money, the team aspect was the ultimate highlight, especially as a young player. "I think the other thing that's important was just the potential to be on the team and be surrounded by other great champions—current and upcoming—and to have kind of a base, so that you weren't out there week to week to week [alone]," she explained.

The transition from athlete to businesswoman with the league came after she was deciding what to do next with her career, especially after being the No.1 doubles player in the world in 1976. Fast forward ten years, and she became the vice president of the league in 1986 and the executive director in 1991.

"I thought it'd be a great way to transition," said Kloss. "I guess I didn't really realize how much I loved it, and that maybe I had some of my dad's DNA. He was a salesman. Because I played, it really had given me an insight to how players think and some of the challenges."

Kloss added that her having played and won at WTT and then joining as an executive was a welcome case for her involved athlete colleagues. "I was able to relate to players which was helpful."

And since rising in the ranks and taking control of the league since 2001, she talked about her leadership skills. "I like to have a team approach. That's my nature," she said. "I think when you work for a small company, chip in and it does become more like a family."

Kloss added: "There are pros and cons to that. I think at the end of the day you have to listen, get everyone's opinion, but when you're the team captain or the coach, the ultimate decision and responsibility rests with me. But, I do look at it as a team."

**

With a new champion crowned for the league in 2001 over the Capitals, the next season the most successful team in league history ended up recruiting one of the strongest American male players ever: Andre Agassi. He signed on for three years, according to the terms of the deal.

When Agassi signed up to play for WTT, he also came up with an integral change to the league's format. Before 2002, the order of play was preset as doubles, singles, doubles, singles, doubles. When Andre signed on, he asked why WTT didn't let the home teams determine the order of play since every game counted anyway. However, there was no reason to dictate to teams that the night end with doubles, especially if the strongest set was singles. Ever since, the home team has determined the order of play an hour before the start of the match—and that's how the "Agassi Rule" came into effect.

Nine teams played in the 22nd consecutive season of the league. Agassi, who was named ambassador and spokesperson for WTT, was joined by tennis stars including John McEnroe, Lindsay Davenport, James Blake, Meghann Shaughnessy, Mark Philippoussis, Alexandra Stevenson, and Corina Morariu (who was in her professional comeback after recovering from cancer).

In an article by tennis journalist Joel Drucker, Agassi's decision to join the league was celebrated as a match made in heaven.

"If ever there were two forces in tennis destined to be peas in a pod, it's World TeamTennis and Andre Agassi," he wrote. "Each is passionate about taking tennis to the masses—in many cases to venues that might not be as familiar with the pro game."

"Each is deeply concerned with using tennis as a platform for making an impact in communities and helping others less fortunate," Drucker continued. "And each has a natural aptitude for sparking up athletic competition with a fair share of entertainment value that will in turn build enthusiasm for tennis."

Playing for the Capitals, Agassi was excited to play for the league. "I love what World TeamTennis does," he said in an interview. "It brings tennis to a new set of people, in a way that's unlike anything in the sport."

Of course, while Agassi was making his debut in the league's pro matches, he had already been a part of the WTT family. The reason: he played in seven of the league's All-Star Smash Hits events to benefit the Elton John AIDS Foundation.

The Las Vegas native praised the WTT format ahead of the 2002 season and compared it to his successful Davis Cup career. "Davis Cup, of course, is very important, but in a way you're still just taking care of your own business, trying to win your match and cheering for your teammates," he said.

"But the format of WTT—where every game counts—makes it even more intense," Agassi continued. "I like that challenge of building your way collectively to victory."

The American had just opened his preparatory academy at the time and expressed his excitement to play for Sacramento as well as for the league's format in terms of inspiring communities.

"There's something unique about the fans of Sacramento being able to follow a team over the course of a season," he explained. "It's very different than when a tournament comes to town for just a week."

Agassi added: "You can root for the team in a way that's more fun than just rooting for a single player. It creates a special kind of loyalty."

Andre Agassi competed for the Sacramento Capitals in 2002 to 2004. Photo: CameraworkUSA

Billie Jean King also praised Agassi for his commitment to the league. "Andre Agassi brings passion and focus to everything he does," she said. "His commitment to his tennis is first-rate. And his heart is even bigger than his forehand."

"What more could you want from a World TeamTennis player?" King added.

His play with the Capitals ended up working out in the league, too. The team had won four consecutive titles, after all. In fact, the team advanced to the championship match yet again, where they faced the New York Buzz at the USTA National Tennis Center in the 2002 season.

"Setting out to win the title back in 2002, the Capitals took on the New York Buzz for the championship in front of a lively crowd at the USTA National Tennis Center," wrote Drucker. "After dropping the opening doubles match, 5-2, to the team of Justin Bower [and] Jeff Coetzee, the Capitals rallied behind 17-year-old WTT rookie Ashley Harkleroad. With forceful versatility, Harkleroad smothered Nannie de Villiers in the singles, 5-1, then moved on to partner with Elena Likhovtseva to beat de Villiers and Natasha Zvereva, 5-0."

It came down to doubles with New York already in a 12-6 hole. "In the end, Likhovtseva and Mark Knowles' 5-1 victory over de Villiers [and] Bower clinched the King Trophy."

For the first time in the league's history, a team had won three consecutive titles thanks to the Capitals. Then four in a row. Now the win over New York marked the first time a team had ever won five titles.

"The flow during a team match is fascinating," said Wayne Bryan, the Capitals coach. "A player gets momentum, the crowd gets involved, the other players pick up on it and then the energy and spirit becomes unbelievable."

"It was great to see everyone step up," he added. "New York was a tough opponent, and to earn that win in front of a New York crowd was incredible."

***

The 2003 season marked WTT matches airing on the newly minted Tennis Channel, which started on May 15, just six weeks before the season began. Another new addition to WTT's roster was the start of the "Ready, Set, Racquet!" program for which WTT had helped distribute hundreds of thousands of free junior racquets.

Ten teams played in 2003, with the newly created and league-owned Newport Beach Breakers playing out of Newport Beach, California, with Lindsay Davenport on board. Other top players to join included Andre Agassi for Sacramento, Andy Roddick for St. Louis, Anna Kournikova for Kansas City, and Boris Becker, who was making his WTT debut for the New York Buzz. Another player to join: the teenaged phenom Maria Sharapova with the Delaware Smash.

Anna Kournikova and 2010 Female MVP teamed up for the St. Louis Aces. Photo: CameraworkUSA

"We now number ten teams, and will again strive to present the best level of tennis entertainment and competition," wrote Ilana Kloss to kick off the season in the official magazine. "Proudly, as one who has been involved in the nurturing of our League since its inception, I am thrilled to be able to continue to blend veteran stars with brash, young talent for an exciting tennis mix."

And even more change took place: The league packed up and moved its offices from Chicago, where it had been for years, to New York City for a fresh start.

"We love New York!" wrote Kloss to WTT fans about the move. "It is just over a year since WTT moved its corporate base to the Big Apple, and I'm happy to report things could not be better."

Ahead of the season, Capitals coach Wayne Bryan was confident in his team's success, especially given their dominant performances over the last few years, which included five titles in six years. "Bring 'em on, we'll fight to see who's best in California and the league," he said.

Agassi also looked forward to his second WTT season. "World TeamTennis adds a special dimension to this sport," he said. "I really enjoyed playing last season and think it'll be even more fun this year."

In the final, the Sacramento Capitals once again advanced to within reach of the King Trophy. However, a motivated Delaware Smash proved to be better that day, taking their first title 21-14 in Flushing Meadows, New York, at the home of the US Open with the help of Liezel Huber, Paul Goldstein, and Samantha Reeves.

The 2004 season began with talented players, including Andre Agassi, Patrick Rafter, Anna Kournikova, and Maria Sharapova (the recent winner at Wimbledon).

New sponsor Advanta joined WTT to begin their "Ready, Set, Racquet" program, handing out thousands of free racquets to juniors in the first year alone.

In her letter to fans, Kloss wrote, "As one who has proudly watched our ten teams develop over the years into a powerhouse of tennis entertainment and competition, I can honestly say that this season will be no different."

She added: "Our players will again strive to leave their very best on the court. We will continue to offer a blend of veteran stars and young, exciting talent in an unconventional format designed to encourage maximum audience participation and a whole lot of fun!"

Kloss continued that the top draft pick for the season was Patrick Rafter, who was signed to the Philadelphia Freedoms. Andre Agassi, meanwhile, joined the Sacramento Capitals for another season in the third year of his contract as league ambassador and spokesman.

"We are particularly proud to have the entire U.S. Davis Cup Team," added Kloss, "reigning US Open Champion Andy Roddick, Mardy Fish and Mike and Bob Bryan on the WTT courts."

Meanwhile, Martina Navratilova, Monica Seles, Anna Kournikova, and Maria Sharapova also joined for the season.

In the championship match, and what would be the final WTT Championship played at Flushing Meadows, the Delaware Smash once again advanced to the finals, having won the previous year by unseating the Sacramento Capitals. This time, however, they were edged out for the title by the Newport Beach Breakers, who claimed their first King Trophy with a 23-17 victory.

Each year, World TeamTennis teams fight for a chance at winning the King Trophy, named after co-founders Billie Jean King and Larry King. Photo: CameraworkUSA

***

The 2005 season marked a huge milestone for WTT: the 30th year of the league's existence. And the match-ups for the season included some of the best in tennis in the league, which had since expanded to include twelve teams, with new franchises started in Houston and the revival of the Boston Lobsters.

Brian MacPhie, Ilana Kloss and Billie Jean King are seen celebrating the 30th anniversary of World TeamTennis. Photo: World TeamTennis

"The 30th season of World TeamTennis action kicks off with the battle of the Martinas," according to the league's archives. "The first singles match between tennis legend Martina Navratilova and her namesake, former world number one, Martina Hingis." Hingis made a surprise return to professional tennis by signing up to play WTT, too, and proved to be a powerful force on the court in her comeback.

"In her first season, Hingis made quite a statement with one of the most dominant performances in WTT history, only losing one set in the seven matches that she played. Her near-perfect play led the Sportimes to their first Championship victory in 2005, and Hingis was named the MVP of the Championship," according to her player profile on the WTT web site.

The league would include 84 matches in 12 markets across the U.S. that season from July 4 to 24. While Hingis made her debut with WTT, Navratilova was playing her 17th season, and for the Boston Lobsters this time around, a team for which she had first played in 1978.

Joining the top women was Steffi Graf in her WTT debut with the Houston Wranglers for an anticipated match against Anna Kournikova. Other women involved were Venus Williams and Maria Sharapova. For the men, players included John McEnroe, Boris Becker, Mardy Fish, Tommy Haas, and Patrick Rafter among others.

**Steffi Graf signs autographs for the fans after playing for the
Houston Wranglers in 2005. Photo: CameraworkUSA**

In the final, Hingis led her New York Sportimes to the championship match, having defeated the Boston Lobsters with Navratilova on board in their conference semifinals. In the final, which took place in Sacramento, California, the Sportimes claimed the King Trophy with a 21-18 victory over the defending champions, the Newport Beach Breakers.

During the match, Hingis didn't lose a single set during her play in championship weekend, according to USTA Eastern, which covered the New York team's results. "Hingis, who was named the Most Valuable Player of the championship weekend, did not lose one set in either Friday's semifinal win over the Boston Lobsters or in the championship match against Newport Beach," according to an article.

"She accounted for 15 of the Sportimes' 21 points in Saturday's championship. Hingis, who is completing her first season in WTT action, dropped only one set all season, losing to Hartford's Meghann Shaughnessy in the Sportimes' second match of the season," it continued.

"We worked hard all season to get ourselves into this position," Hingis said in an interview after the match. "I was very happy to be part of this team and get them going. I knew when the guys lost the first set of doubles I had to step up and get us a lead."

"Newport Beach opened the match with a convincing 5-2 win in men's doubles with Devin Bowen and Delgado overtaking New York's Morrison and Rajeev Ram," according to USTA Eastern. "In the second set, Hingis easily dispatched of Katerina Bondarenko 5-1 to put the Sportimes up one game leading into the mixed doubles."

With Hingis and Ram playing mixed doubles, the two beat Anastasia Rodionova and Delgado, 5-2. Hingis also played with Jenny Hopkins in women's doubles for another 5-2 victory over Newport Beach against Bondarenko and Rodionova.

The article continued, "New York appeared to be cruising to an easy victory when Newport Beach's Ramon Delgado took the final set, men's singles, with a 5-3 win over Jeff Morrison, forcing the match into Overtime." It added: "Delgado won three straight games in Overtime to bring the match to 20-18, but Morrison finally prevailed in the four game of Overtime to seal the victory and the championship for New York."

"I knew we had a lot of ground to make up going into the final set, but my first priority was to get us into Overtime," Delgado said in an interview. "I knew he might tighten up and when I won the first three games I thought we had a chance to win the match. I was playing one point at a time and having played Overtime before, I knew that if I stuck with it, maybe we could come back. I guess we just came up a little short."

In Overtime, Hingis was sidelined, with her work already completed. "It was so nerve-racking to watch when you can't help out the team," she said about closing out the league's 30th season, and her first as a WTT player. "We were so happy when that final point was over."

WTT FINALS 2001

Philadelphia Freedoms

Springfield Lasers

WTT FINALS 2002

Sacramento Capitals

New York Buzz

WTT FINALS 2003

Delaware Smash

Sacramento Capitals

WTT FINALS 2004

Newport Beach Breakers  23

Delaware Smash 17

WTT FINALS 2005

New York Sportimes 21

Newport Beach Breakers 18

Chapter Seven: Seasons Thirty-One to Thirty-Five (2006-2010):

WTT Turns 35

2006 TEAMS & PLAYERS:

EASTERN CONFERENCE:

Boston Lobsters:	Thomas Blake, Amir Hadad, Todd Martin, Martina Navratilova, Nicole Pratt, Kristen Schlukebir. COACH: Anne Smith
Delaware Smash:	Tres Davis, Angela Haynes, Liezel Huber, Eric Nunez. COACH: Mariaan De Swardt
Hartford FoxForce:	Goran Dragicevic, Lisa McShea, Meghann Shaughnessy, Abigail Spears, Glenn Weiner. COACH: Don Johnson
New York Buzz:	KC Corkery, Julie Ditty, Viktoriya Kutuzova, Scott Lipsky. COACH: Jolene Watanabe
New York Sportimes:	Alex Bogomolov, Jr., Ashley Harkleroad, Martina Hingis, David Martin, John McEnroe, Vladka Uhlirova. COACH: Chuck Adams
Philadelphia Freedoms:	Jaymon Crabb, Casey Dellacqua, Daniel Nestor, Frederic Niemeyer, Lisa Raymond, Rennae Stubbs, Venus Williams. COACH: Craig Kardon

WESTERN CONFERENCE:

Houston Wranglers:	Mardy Fish, Jan-Michael Gambill, Anna-Lena Groenefeld, Graydon Oliver, Ahsha Rolle, Bryanne Stewart. COACH: Jim Mavity
Kansas City Explorers:	Bob Bryan, Mike Bryan, David Macpherson, Brian MacPhie, Corina Morariu, Caroline Wozniacki. COACH: Kirkland Gates
Newport Beach Breakers:	Ramon Delgado, Tina Krizan, Rick Leach, Anastasia Rodionova, Pete Sampras. COACH: Dick Leach
Sacramento Capitals:	Mark Knowles, Anna Kournikova, Elena Likhovtseva, Anastasia Pavlyuchenkova, Abigail Spears, Nicole Vaidisova, Sam Warburg. COACH: Wayne Bryan
St. Louis Aces:	John Paul Fruttero, Maria Emilia Salerni, Aleke Tsoubanos, Brian Wilson. COACH: Greg Patton
Springfield Lasers:	Victoria Azarenka, Nick Monroe, Anastasia Myskina, Andreea Vanc, Aleksandar Vlaski. COACH: Trevor Kronemann
WTT FINALS *(in Newport Beach, Calif.):*	Philadelphia Freedoms def. Newport Beach Breakers 21-14

2007 TEAMS & PLAYERS:
EASTERN CONFERENCE:

Boston Lobsters:	Julie Ditty, Christina Fusano, Amir Hadad, Nikita Kryvonos, Arantxa Sanchez-Vicario. COACH: Anne Smith
Delaware Smash:	Lester Cook, Chris Haggard, Angela Haynes, Liezel Huber. COACH: Mariaan de Swardt
New York Buzz:	Greta Arn, Rik DeVoest, Ashley Fisher, Gabriela Navratilova. COACH: Jolene Watanabe
New York Sportimes:	Ashley Harkleroad, John McEnroe, Mirko Pehar, Hana Sromova, Jesse Witten. COACH: Chuck Adams
Philadelphia Freedoms:	Jamea Jackson, Daniel Nestor, Fred Niemeyer, Travis Parrott, Lisa Raymond, Olga Savchuk, Venus Williams. COACH: Craig Kardon

WESTERN CONFERENCE:

Houston Wranglers:	Goran Dragicevic, Jan-Michael Gambill, Bryanne Stewart, Mashona Washington. COACH: Thomas Blake
Kansas City Explorers:	Bob Bryan, Mike Bryan, Jarmila Gajdosova, David Macpherson, Corina Morariu, Dusan Vemic. COACH: Brent Haygarth
Newport Beach Breakers:	Lauren Albanese, Ramon Delgado, Rick Leach, Michaela Pastikova, Pete Sampras, Maria Sharapova, Jeff Tarango. COACH: Trevor Kronemann
Sacramento Capitals:	Lindsay Davenport, Mark Knowles, Anna Kournikova, Michelle Larcher de Brito, Elena Likhovtseva, Sam Warburg. COACH: Wayne Bryan
Springfield Lasers:	Todd Perry, Tamarine Tanasugarn, Andreea Vanc, Martin Verkerk, Glenn Weiner. COACH: John-Laffnie de Jager
St. Louis Aces:	Jonathan Erlich, Nick Rainey, Andy Ram, Aleke Tsoubanos, Brian Wilson, Jasmin Woehr. COACH: Sean Cole
WTT FINALS (in Sacramento, Calif.):	Sacramento Capitals def. New York Buzz, 24-20 OT

2008 TEAMS & PLAYERS:
EASTERN CONFERENCE:

Boston Lobsters:	Jan-Michael Gambill, Amir Hadad, Raquel Kops-Jones, Martina Navratilova, Marie-Eve Pelletier. COACH: Tim Mayotte
Delaware Smash:	Madison Brengle, Josh Cohen, Ryler De Heart, Christina Fusano, Chris Haggard, Liezel Huber. COACH: Mariaan de Swardt
New York Buzz:	Patrick Briaud, Nathan Healey, Gabriela Navratilova, Yaraslava Shvedova. COACH: Jay Udwadia
New York Sportimes:	Bethanie Mattek, John McEnroe, Milagros Sequera, Hana Sromova, Brian Wilson, Jesse Witten. COACH: Dustin Taylor

Philadelphia Freedoms:	Alex Bogomolov, Audra Cohen, Travis Parrott, Lisa Raymond, Venus Williams. COACH: Craig Kardon
Washington Kastles:	Justin Gimelstob, Sacha Jones, Scott Oudsema, Mashona Washington, Serena Williams. COACH: Thomas Blake

WESTERN CONFERENCE:

Kansas City Explorers:	James Auckland, Bob Bryan, Mike Bryan, Kveta Peschke, Rennae Stubbs, Dusan Vemic. COACH: Brent Haygarth
Newport Beach Breakers:	Angelika Bachmann, Rebecca Bernhard, Lindsay Davenport, Ramon Delgado, Lilia Osterloh, Michaela Pastikova, Kaes Van't Hof. COACH: Trevor Kronemann
Sacramento Capitals:	Eric Butorac, Tamaryn Hendler, Elena Likhovtseva, Dmitry Tursunov, Sam Warburg. COACH: Wayne Bryan
Springfield Lasers:	Shenay Perry, Todd Perry, Chanelle Scheepers, Isak Van der Merwe, Glenn Weiner. COACH: John-Laffnie de Jager
St. Louis Aces:	Uladzimir Ignatik, Anna Kournikova, Jelena Pandzic, Sam Querrey, Travis Rettenmaier, Jasmine Woehr. COACH: Greg Patton
WTT FINALS *(in Sacramento, Calif.)*:	New York Buzz def. Kansas City Explorers 21-18

2009 TEAMS & PLAYERS:
EASTERN CONFERENCE:

Boston Lobsters:	James Auckland, Stephanie Foretz, Jan-Michael Gambill, Raquel Kops-Jones, Martina Navratilova. COACH: Bud Schultz
New York Buzz:	Mallory Burdette, Alex Domijan, Matthew Kandath, Jack Sock, Sloane Stephens, Allie Will, COACH: Roger Smith
New York Sportimes:	Christina Fusano, Robert Kendrick, John McEnroe, Abigail Spears, Jesse Witten. COACH: Chuck Adams
Philadelphia Freedoms:	Andre Agassi, Nathan Healey, Madison Keys, Travis Parrott, Lisa Raymond, Venus Williams, Eric Nunez. COACH: Craig Kardon
Washington Kastles:	Scott Oudsema, Leander Paes, Nadia Petrova, Olga Puchkova, Rennae Stubbs, Serena Williams. COACH: Murphy Jensen

WESTERN CONFERENCE:

Kansas City Explorers:	Eugenie Bouchard, Bob Bryan, Mike Bryan, Kveta Peschke, Mike Russell, Dusan Vemic, Tara Snyder, Lindsay Lee Waters. COACH: Brent Haygarth
Newport Beach Breakers:	Ramon Delgado, Julie Ditty, Marie-Eve Pelletier, Maria Sharapova, Kaes Van't Hof. COACH: Trevor Kronemann
Sacramento Capitals:	Michael Chang, Angela Haynes, Mark Knowles, CoCo Vandeweghe, Sam Warburg. COACH: Wayne Bryan

Springfield Lasers:	Martin Damm, Liezel Huber, Vania King, Raven Klaasen, Chanelle Scheepers. COACH: John-Laffnie de Jager
St. Louis Aces:	Kim Clijsters, Liga Dekmeijere, Mislav Hizak, Anna Kournikova, Tripp Phillips, Sam Querrey, Ashley Weinhold. COACH: Roger Follmer
WTT FINALS (in Washington, DC):	Washington Kastles def. Springfield Lasers, 23-20

2010 TEAMS & PLAYERS:
EASTERN CONFERENCE:

Boston Lobsters:	James Blake, Eric Butorac, Jan-Michael Gambill, John Isner, Raquel Kops-Jones, CoCo Vandeweghe. COACH: Bud Schultz
New York Buzz:	Sarah Borwell, Alex Domijan, Scoville Jenkins, Martina Hingis. COACH: Jay Udwadia
New York Sportimes:	Kim Clijsters, Ashley Harkleroad, Robert Kendrick, John McEnroe, Abigail Spears, Jesse Witten. COACH: Chuck Adams
Philadelphia Freedoms:	Prakash Amritraj, Ramon Delgado, Noppawan Lertcheewakarn, Courtney Nagle, Andy Roddick. COACH: Craig Kardon. ASSISTANT COACH: Josh Cohen
Washington Kastles:	Angela Haynes, Leander Paes, Bobby Reynolds, Rennae Stubbs, Serena Williams, Venus Williams. COACH: Murphy Jensen

WESTERN CONFERENCE:

Kansas City Explorers:	Jarmila Groth, Samuel Groth, Ricardo Mello, Kveta Peschke, Bob Bryan, Mike Bryan. COACH: Brent Haygarth
Newport Beach Breakers:	Lester Cook, Julie Ditty, David Martin, Marie-Eve Pelletier, Maria Sharapova. COACH: Trevor Kronemann
Sacramento Capitals:	Michael Chang, Brett Joelson, Vania King, Mark Knowles, Dusan Vemic, Riza Zalameda. COACH: Wayne Bryan
Springfield Lasers:	Martin Damm, Carly Gullickson, Chanelle Scheepers, Rik De Voest. COACH: John-Laffnie de Jager
St. Louis Aces:	Lindsay Davenport, Liga Dekmeijere, Andrei Pavel, Anna Kournikova, Tripp Phillips. COACH: Rick Leach
WTT FINALS (in Kansas City, Mo):	KANSAS CITY EXPLORERS def. New York Sportimes, 21-18

The 30th anniversary came to a close in thrilling fashion with Martina Hingis' performance at championship weekend. Moreover, the last five years saw the league filled with some of the most legendary players of all time. But the league also grew its recreational league further, while reaching more markets and communities in which to grow the game of tennis.

Meanwhile, the next five seasons, from 2006 to 2010, saw the beginnings of another dominant franchise in a similar fashion to the Sacramento Capitals' run: the Washington Kastles.

In the 2006 season, the first overall draft pick was a familiar name to tennis fans everywhere: Pete Sampras, one of the greatest of all time. He was selected by the Newport Beach Breakers. Venus Williams, meanwhile, was traded to the Philadelphia Freedoms.

As the season commenced, the first semifinal took place on July 29 with the Philadelphia Freedoms taking on the New York Sportimes. The Philadelphia Freedoms would ultimately advance thanks to Lisa Raymond upping her level and dominating in doubles with partner Rennae Stubbs.

"Lisa Raymond played the best match of the year tonight," said the Freedoms coach Craig Kardon about her performance after the match concluded. "It's good to have a player who can come through in the clutch."

The Freedoms barely even made it to the semis, though. In fact, they qualified on the last night of the regular season, according to the league's archives. "We're excited about getting to the finals," said Raymond after the victory. "I played my best match this season. Our whole team came out fired up and we played great as a team."

"Raymond and Stubbs opened the match with a well-played women's doubles win over Cara Black and Ashley Harkleroad, 5-3," according to a match report. "Raymond used the momentum from the opening set to oust Harkleroad in singles, winning 5-2."

But the New York team wouldn't just roll over for their opponents. "The Sportimes kept in the match with a close 5-4 win by Alex Bogomolov, Jr., over the Freedoms' Jaymon Crabb," reported the article. "Bogomolov finally prevailed in a tiebreaker, winning 5-4 (4)."

Philadelphia kept going, with Daniel Nestor and Stubbs claiming mixed doubles 5-2. Although men's doubles went the way of New York to force the match into Overtime, it was Philadelphia on top by claiming a 23-17 victory and the place in the finals.

In the other semifinal, the Newport Beach Breakers advanced to another WTT final in surprising fashion over the top-seeded Sacramento Capitals. "Despite getting blown out in the first set, 5-0, the Newport Beach Breakers continued their surprising run in the WTT Playoffs, coming from behind to oust the top-seeded Sacramento Capitals 19-18 in World TeamTennis action Saturday in Newport Beach," according to a match report from the archives.

To kick things off, Mark Knowles and Elena Likhovtseva secured a 5-0 win over Tina Krizan and Rick Leach. But Newport Beach rallied in women's singles with Anastasia Rodionova beating Likhovtseva 5-2.

"Sacramento bounced back in men's singles when Sam Warburg held off the Breakers' Ramon Delgado in a tiebreaker, 5-4 (3)," it continued. "Not willing to go away quietly, the Breakers rallied in women's doubles with Rodionova and Krizan going to another tiebreaker to oust Likhovtseva and Anastasia Pavlyuchenkova 5-4 (1)."

The Breakers made the comeback a reality when Delgado and Leach defeated Knowles and Warburg in men's doubles, 5-2.

"We all played really well today," Delgado said after the match. "I am so happy we played so well in doubles to close out the match."

He added: "It was really unbelievable that we came back to win the match without having to go to Overtime. All day long the whole team stayed together on every point in every game."

The championship match began for the Newport Beach team with Ramon Delgado taking a 5-3 set over Jaymon Crabb of Philadelphia. "The momentum swung to the Freedoms when Raymond and Rennae Stubbs overpowered the Breakers' Anastasia Rodionova and Tina Krizan 5-1 in women's doubles to give Philadelphia an early lead," according to the match report.

But in men's doubles, the Breakers evened the match at 11-all at halftime as Delgado and Rick Leach upset Daniel Nestor and Crabb, 5-3.

Meanwhile, Lisa Raymond of Philadelphia defeated Rodionova 5-3 to help the Freedoms to a 16-14 lead for the final set.

"Rodionova played well all day," Raymond said. "At the end [of women's singles] I just was able to run everything down and I fought a little harder because I knew I needed to give us some cushion heading into the final set."

Philadelphia easily won their mixed doubles match over Newport by not letting the Breakers win a game in the last set. The win meant the Freedoms' second championship title in WTT, closing out their opposition 21-14 for the King Trophy. They also won the title in 2001.

"Daniel and I have played well together all season," Stubbs said. "Lisa gave us a nice cushion and once we got the first break, we felt we could roll through the set. We knew when we got to Newport Beach there was no looking back and I think we earned the title this weekend."

"We got a little help from some other teams to get us into the Finals," said Craig Kardon, the coach of the Freedoms, after the match. "But, once we got here, we took control of things. We have some of the finest players in the world on our team and they did not disappoint anyone this weekend."

***

The 2007 season was marked by star power, including two wildly popular female players: Maria Sharapova and Serena Williams. "Sharapova, currently ranked No. 2 in the world, will play for the Newport Beach Breakers on Monday, July 16, when they host the Kansas City Explorers," according to the league's archives. "Sharapova previously played three seasons for the Breakers from 2003-2005. She made her WTT debut as a teenager in 2002 for the Delaware Smash.

**Maria Sharapova, who has played seven seasons of World TeamTennis, teaches
a young fan during a Breakers home match. Photo: CameraworkUSA**

Meanwhile, Serena Williams was returning to World TeamTennis for the first time since her debut in 2000. She was set to play for the St. Louis Aces at the time.

Others to play in the season were Venus Williams, Pete Sampras, Anna Kournikova, John McEnroe, and Mike and Bob Bryan.

Venus, who was playing in her fourth season for the league, talked to reporters ahead of her second season with the Freedoms. "I enjoy it, have fun. I love playing on the team with the people I play on the team with. I love playing with Lisa Raymond," she said. "We just played in Fed Cup this weekend. In general, I just have a great time. It's a great way to play tennis and really enjoy the moment."

Davenport, meanwhile, agreed to play WTT again just six weeks after giving birth to her first child. She played for the Sacramento Capitals, the team she played with in 1993; this was her first time playing in the league since 2003. Davenport discussed her decision to play again after the birth of her son.

"Yeah, you know, Ilana is a friend of mine. We have been obviously in contact through my pregnancy," she said. "You know, originally Jagger was not due until July 2nd, so I told her it probably wasn't going to be likely, knowing when the TeamTennis season was. But because of some complications we had with him, he actually came obviously three weeks early on June 10th."

Davenport added, "I talked to her shortly after and said, 'I'm feeling great. You know, I think I'll be ready to do it.'" She continued, "I looked at it really as kind of a fun challenge to see, you know, if I could come back so quickly and kind of get me a little kick in the pants to get back being active, you know, being healthy and all of that stuff."

Fast forward to the tail end of the season, and the Western Conference Championship match took place. Davenport's team advanced to the final four for a shot at yet another King Trophy, which would be their record sixth.

"Springfield faced off against the strength of the Capitals' lineup in the opening set, taking on one of the League's top doubles teams in Mark Knowles and Sam Warburg. Back-to-back aces from Warburg put the Caps up 4-2 before a lob winner by Knowles closed out the first set 5-2," according to a match report from the league's archives.

Warburg defeated Martin Verkerk 5-3, while Knowles continued a winning streak in mixed doubles with Elena Likhovtseva to take a 5-3 victory over Glenn Weiner and Andreea Vanc.

"Trailing 15-8 at halftime, Springfield went to the heart of their lineup for two matches with two of the strongest women in the League-Tamarine Tanasugarn and Andreea Vanc," the report added. "Tanasugarn, who was named WTT Female MVP prior to the match, started strong by breaking Likhovtseva's serve in the first game." But Likhovtseva grabbed the early 2-1 lead before Tanasugarn broke back to go up 3-2. Ultimately, Tanasugarn broke Likhovtseva's serve and closed out "the set 5-3 for the Lasers' only win of the night."

"Down by five points going into the final set, the Lasers fielded the top doubles team in the League but it was Sacramento that broke serve in the first game. The 14-year-old Michelle Larcher de Brito of Sacramento may be the youngest player in WTT history, but she showed poise during the women's doubles set to get out to a 2-0 lead," according to the match report. "Tanasugarn and Vanc rallied to a 3-2 lead before the momentum swung back to the Caps. Two volley winners from Likhovtseva in the tiebreaker propelled the Caps to a 5-4 victory and the Western Conference title."

With the win, the Capitals took out the Lasers 23-17 in front of over 3,000 fans.

"Playing at home was great, especially against the best team in the League," said Knowles after the win and after being named the WTT Male MVP of the Year. "We had a great crowd and they really pushed us through it. Men's doubles got us off to a good start and Sam backed it up in men's singles. It was a great night for the Caps."

In the Eastern Conference Championship, the New York Buzz upset the defending champion, Philadelphia Freedoms, in a close 20-19 victory.

"I knew from the start that I was playing the last set and I was excited that it would come down to me to hopefully win the match," said De Voest about the win. "I've had a lot of close matches with Freddy [Niemeyer] and I just wanted it to be close when we got to the last set as I usually play well against him."

He added, "The key to the match was staying upbeat and having positive energy, even when we were down."

To try to advance to the championship round, the Freedoms claimed a 10-6 lead after two sets by winning mixed doubles and women's doubles. "The Freedoms' Daniel Nestor and Lisa Raymond teamed up for a 5-3 win in mixed doubles over De Voest and Greta Arn of New York. Raymond and Olga Savchuk were too much for Greta Arn and Gabriela Navratilova in women's doubles, taking the second set 5-3," according to the article covering the win.

But the Buzz won men's doubles 5-2, bringing New York within one point of victory at halftime, 12-11.

Women's singles was decided in a tiebreaker when Greta Arn double-faulted to give Savchuk a 5-4 (3) win and the Freedoms a two-point lead going into the final set of men's singles.

"Rik de Voest rallied the Buzz with a 5-2 singles win over Frederic Niemeyer in the final set," according to a match report. "De Voest broke Niemeyer's serve in the fourth game to go up 3-1 and bring the Buzz even at 18-18. Niemeyer held off one match point to hold serve at 4-2, but it wasn't enough as De Voest served out the set 5-2 to send the Buzz to the WTT Finals."

In the final, the Sacramento Capitals went on to claim their record sixth league title over the New York Buzz in captivating fashion. Meanwhile, it was the third time the New York Buzz lost to the Caps in a championship match for the King Trophy.

"After opening the 2007 season with two losses, the Caps won 11 of their final 12 matches to advance to the WTT Championship on their home court in Roseville. Home court was an advantage for the Caps with boisterous support from most of the 4,112 fans who packed the stands for the finals and brought their air horns, Caps signs and cow bells," according to a match report.

The Buzz started the match by breaking Elena Likhovtseva's serve to go up 2-1 in the first set, although the Capitals returned it by breaking Greta Arn's serve to get even at 2-2. "Arn's serving problems continued as she double faulted at 4-4 in the tiebreaker to give the Caps a narrow 5-4 win in mixed doubles," according to the official match report.

"Likhovtseva kept the momentum in the Caps' court in women's singles. The eight-year Caps veteran aced Arn then followed up with a backhand winner on game point to go up 3-2. Likhovtseva closed out the set 5-3," the article continued.

"Today was my best match so far," said Likhovtseva about her play. "I wasn't nervous and I had great support from my teammates and the crowd. It was a great night."

"Rik de Voest carried the Buzz into the WTT Finals with his singles performance in the Eastern Conference Championship match on Saturday, but it was the big-serving Sam Warburg who stole the show in men's singles during the Finals," said the match report. Warburg beat De Voest 5-4(1). "I knew playing Rik would be a tough challenge but I was focused on my game plan and it worked," said Warburg in an interview.

Michelle Larcher de Brito (the youngest WTT player ever) and Likhovtseva won the opening game of women's doubles. "New York's woes continued with miscommunication between Arn and Navratilova as Larcher de Brito's shot dropped untouched between the two to give Sacramento a quick 2-0 lead," according to the article. "It wasn't enough as the Buzz broke Larcher de Brito's serve to send the set into a tiebreaker." Likhovtseva took the tiebreaker 5-0 thanks to a volley winner, giving Sacramento a 5-4 win and a 20-15 lead going into the final set of the season.

"The League's top two men's doubles teams faced off in the fifth set and the action lived up to their billing. The teams traded service breaks in the first two games before 2007 League MVP Knowles held serve to put the Caps up 2-1," according to the match report. "De Voest and Ashley Fisher posted a 5-3 win to send the match into Overtime. The Caps rebounded quickly as Warburg held serve in the first game of Overtime to give the Caps their sixth WTT title."

"The crowd was unbelievable," said Sam Warburg about the win. "Playing at home really helped us, the support was great." Warburg celebrated the win by drenching Wayne Bryan, the team's coach, with the contents of a Gatorade cooler.

The Sacramento Capitals defeated the New York Buzz to become the league champions
for the sixth time in 2007. Pictured (l. to r.): Elena Likhovtseva, Mark Knowles, Michelle
Larcher de Brito, Sam Warburg and coach Wayne Bryan. Photo: CameraworkUSA

***

Ahead of the 2008 season, the 33rd year of WTT, a change was made in the way the WTT Championship Weekend was decided. According to an announcement by the league in November: "For the 2008 season, five teams will advance to the WTT Championship Weekend, July 25-27, to battle for the King Trophy. The top two teams from both the Eastern and Western Conferences automatically qualify for the playoffs. WTT is adding a wild card match that will feature the No. 4 seed and a wild card team." The announcement continued, "The wild card will either be the host team or the team with the fifth best overall League record (if the host team qualifies as one of the top two teams from their conference)."

Another big thing happened for the 2008 season: the Washington Kastles franchise began, led by owner Mark Ein. "Washington DC is a world-class sports market that will be a showcase for World TeamTennis," said Kloss in the announcement.

She added: "We've looked at this market for several years as a great location for expansion. Thanks to the leadership and vision of Mark Ein, everything came together for it to happen this year."

"Area fans have supported tennis for many years and we think they will really embrace our unique brand of tennis," she said.

"I am thrilled to bring World TeamTennis to our area. WTT tennis is great entertainment emphasizing fan interaction, and it is the only major sport with men and women playing together on the same team," said Ein at the time. "The Washington Kastles season will be an exciting summertime addition to our local economy and a fun activity for our entire community."

As the season got ready to kick off, and with the new franchise settled, players expressed their excitement to be part of the league for another season. League veteran Anna Kournikova was just one of the players rejoining for the 3rd season. This time, the Russian would be playing in her sixth year of World TeamTennis and for the St. Louis Aces.

In a conference call, Kournikova discussed what keeps her coming back to the league. "Well, for me, oh, my God, there's a million reasons. It's my sixth season playing. Obviously I'm not on the professional tour, so for me this is the best opportunity I can get to be on the tennis court, to be in the match environment, to be in front of my fans, to be just part of such a great league," she said to reporters.

"WTT is awesome. It's a perfect environment for the fans to see singles, doubles, and women's, mixed, everything. I mean, it couldn't be better. I wouldn't miss it for the world," she added. "I'm really looking forward to being back on the court. I love those moments obviously. I miss playing. But I love just now playing for fun and really enjoying myself out there on the court."

With the new format being used to determine the players in the WTT championship match, the first semifinal saw the Kansas City Explorers compete against the six-time league champions, the Sacramento Capitals.

"The Explorers dominated the three doubles, losing only four games in the final three events. WTT Female MVP Rennae Stubbs paired with Dusan Vemic to defeat Sacramento's Elena Likhovtseva and Eric Butorac 5-3 in the mixed doubles," according to the league's archives. "Stubbs then teamed with Kveta Peschke to blank Likhovtseva and Tammy Hendler in the women's doubles, winning 5-0. In men's doubles, Kansas City's James Auckland and Vemic won easily, taking out Sam Warburg and Butorac, 5-1."

Sacramento won just one set over the course of the night: the opening set, with Warburg beating Vemic 5-1 in men's singles. Meanwhile, in women's singles, Peschke took out Likhovtseva 5-1. Although Sacramento substituted Likhovtseva for Hendler at 1-3, she failed to win the set.

"We faced a much different Caps team than we did the first week of the season," said Kansas City coach Brent Haygarth after the match. "Tonight we changed the order of play, relying on our doubles teams in case we got down early. It worked in our favor, and we were able to get on top of the match starting with the second event."

"The Explorers posted the best record in the League this season, finishing 13-1. Friday's win was the third time this season the Explorers defeated Sacramento," reported the article.

With the victory, Kansas City advanced to the Sunday final, which was being decided between the New York Buzz and the New York Sportimes.

"Our only loss of the season was to the Buzz, but regardless of who wins on Saturday, we will be ready," Haygarth said after the victory. "It will help to be the home team on Sunday and being able to set the line-up will be a huge advantage because, in the WTT format, every point is important."

In that semi between the two New York franchises, it was the New York Buzz to advance to the championship round. They defeated the Sportimes squad with John McEnroe in tow by 25-17 in Overtime.

"The Buzz swept four of the five events in Saturday's semifinal. The Buzz took both singles events with WTT Female Rookie of the Year Yaroslava Shvedova ousting Ashley Harkleroad 5-2 in Women's Singles and Nathan Healey defeating Jesse Witten 5-2 in Men's Singles," said the match report.

The Buzz won women's doubles as well as mixed doubles by 5-4 and 5-3 scores.

"The Sportimes picked up their only win of the night in men's doubles when McEnroe and Witten defeated Healey and Patrick Briaud 5-4 and forced the match into Overtime. Healey and Briaud won the second game of extended play and sealed the victory for the Buzz," the report added.

In the championship match, the New York Buzz was attempting to win their first title in 14 years and in four different attempts against the Kansas City Explorers.

During the match, the Buzz started strong by winning the two singles sets with Nathan Healey taking out Dusan Vemic 5-3 in men's singles and Yaroslava Shvedova taking a 5-3 win over Kveta Peschke. That got the Buzz to a 10-6 lead to kick off play.

"Kansas City closed the gap to 13-11 at halftime after Rennae Stubbs and Vemic scored a 5-3 mixed doubles win over Healey and Shvedova," according to the league's archives. "Stubbs and Peschke then secured a 5-3 win over Shvedova and Gabriela Navratilova in women's doubles."

The match was then tied at 16-all with play heading into the final event of the 2008 season. "Healey and Patrick Briaud came up strong to close out the match, defeating the Explorers' James Auckland and Vemic 5-2," according to the match report. "The match ended on a point when Vemic touched the net to seal the victory and the first WTT crown for the Buzz."

"We played really well in the last set and even if Vemic had not touched the net, we were prepared to serve for the match at the end," Healey said in an interview after the match. "After more than three weeks on the road and playing a lot of matches, it feels great to win the whole thing."

"We knew from the time we drafted this team, we were going to win this year," said Nitty Singh, the New York Buzz's owner. "This championship has been a long time coming and things worked out well for us this year. From relocating the team to a new site in Albany to having a team that wanted to win so badly and were willing to set everything aside to accomplish that goal, we knew we had something special."

Singh added, "We felt it was our year, our destiny."

The New York Buzz beat the Kansas City Explorers in the 2008 final to claim the King Trophy. Pictured (l. to r.): WTT CEO/Commissioner Ilana Kloss, Yaroslava Shvedova, Gabriela Navratilova, Nathan Healey, Patrick Briaud, Coach Jay Udwadia, Advanta representative David Goodman and team owner Nitty Singh. Photo: CameraworkUSA

***

Highlight #7: World TeamTennis and the USTA Partnership

The 2009 season began with another large announcement, similar in many ways to the new franchise beginning in Washington. To start the year in January, the league, with its title sponsor as Advanta, said that the United States Tennis Association would become a 25 percent owner in the league in order to market its initiatives and grow its recreational league for juniors.

"One of the main goals in the new partnership is to provide an expanded marketing platform for the USTA's Jr. TeamTennis Program through the Advanta World TeamTennis Pro League teams and players," said a press release at the time. "The Jr. TeamTennis program is a recreational tennis league for children ages 6 – 18, and features the USTA's QuickStart format for children under the age of 10." The USTA's Jr. TeamTennis was established in 1991 and had over 80,000 participants at the time.

"In each of the franchise markets, Advanta WTT Pro League teams and USTA sections will work together on youth initiatives to broaden the reach of QuickStart and Jr. TeamTennis programs. These recreational efforts are becoming integrated with the WTT professional franchises to encourage more young children to take up tennis as a team sport," said the release.

It continued, "Jr. TeamTennis leagues are expected to contest some of their playoff and championship matches on the same multi-colored courts used by the WTT pro teams and will also have the opportunity to interact with many of the top players who compete in the Pro League."

"By working with the USTA, we will take World TeamTennis to the next level in the U.S.," said King about the partnership. "We've been looking for an opportunity like this for a long time and I can't think of a better partner than the USTA. I'm excited about what the future holds for our partnership."

"We are thrilled to be once again teaming with one of the greatest ambassadors in tennis, Billie Jean King," said Lucy S. Garvin, the chairman of the Board and president of the USTA at the time. "The USTA recognizes the reciprocal relationship between the pro game and grassroots play, and our new partnership with World TeamTennis provides us a natural platform to promote our many youth initiatives including Jr. TeamTennis."

"Our vision is to grow tennis at every level across the country," said Kloss. "We believe the WTT team format can be one of the building blocks to do that. The Advanta WTT Pro League connects professional players and communities in a unique way and can inspire kids to take up tennis as a team sport."

She added, "That's an initiative our pro team owners can build on by working with the USTA and the sections to showcase great youth-oriented programs like QuickStart and Junior TeamTennis."

Katrina Adams, who began serving as the USTA president in 2015 and who played for WTT for five seasons during the 1990s, recalled: "For me, during that time period, it was a lot of fun. The opportunity to play with guys and a couple women for a month straight, traveling, having a great time living through the ups and downs, dealing with the challenges of late night travel and waking up to have to play the next day," she said. "It was a lot of lessons learned in how to manage myself individually, but also to be able to support your teammates in the toughness of crunch time."

Adams also spoke about the Tennis on Campus initiative the USTA partnered with WTT on to give college-age tennis players a chance to compete in the format. "Not every tennis player is going to earn a collegiate scholarship and you often have players that could earn a collegiate scholarship but chose to go to a college or university of their choice and not play tennis, based on what their academic track is and what their endeavors are," she said. "These colleges and universities now have a club team of which these players can go and play competitively on a less stress stage and still get their competitive juices taken care of."

Adams continued, "The numbers I think have truly skyrocketed because there are thousands of young players that are like that, or just don't want to play varsity tennis beyond their competitive days in high school or on the junior circuit, but they can still play."

She discussed the ability to work with King, too, both through WTT and as USTA president. "I mean we all know what Billie Jean stands for and who she is and what she brings to the table with her energy, her vision, being innovative, being a mentor, and really being a leader in women's sports, not just tennis," she explained. "When you have someone like that who is your friend, who's on your side, who I can reach out and call at any given time, just to run things by her or just to listen to her wisdom, is a huge asset for me in my leadership role, but obviously of whom, naming the USTA Billie Jean King National Tennis Center after her, shows the respect that we have for who she is and what she has accomplished."

Glenn Arrington, who has headed up the Tennis on Campus program with World TeamTennis' Elaine Wingfield, also discussed the format. "I call it the perfect storm; we have been lucky that over the last 20 years there's been a huge explosion of club sports on college campuses for all the students on college campuses to take part and enjoy themselves and the World TeamTennis format because of particularly the co-ed nature and the fact that it allowed you to compete—boys and girls—on a team," he said. The fact that girls and boys can play singles and doubles then allows each match to "crescendo" to a mixed doubles team.

He added that Billie Jean King's legacy with World TeamTennis is something of which he's proud to be part. "To have her available to come to our events and meet with the kids to share sportsmanship ideals and leadership ideals with the kids is really amazing," he said. "It is a pretty big deal. You think it's just a format but it's tried and tested and gone through a lot of scrutiny."

Arrington added, "I am just really proud that Kurt [Kamperman, a USTA executive] had the vision to really work on a collaboration with the [WTT] and I got to be the person to help facilitate that relationship at least through this network."

He said, "That has been cool for me in my career."

***

Later in January, meanwhile, the Delaware Smash announced that it would be shutting down operations and would not be playing in the 2009 season. General manager Jeff Harrison made the announcement, citing a lack of a presenting sponsor as a prime reason for it focusing instead on community tennis efforts.

"Given our long history with tennis in Wilmington and the region, this decision was very difficult, especially from an emotional standpoint," said King. "But from a business position, we were left with only one choice. There are terrific fans here and we've had a great run and winning the title in 2003 was definitely one of my favorite WTT moments. We want to stay involved with tennis in the Wilmington area and keep Delaware fans connected to World TeamTennis."

"It's always hard to lose any team, but we understand the ownership decision as it's important that teams are successful from both a community and business standpoint," said Kloss. "We are extremely pleased that WTT will continue to have a presence in the market with the continuing grassroots initiatives."

Meanwhile, in other franchise news, the New York Sportimes moved their operations to New York City from Mamaroneck. This marked the first time World TeamTennis would be in the Big Apple in more than thirty years, according to *The New York Times*.

In terms of players, Serena Williams and Andre Agassi were those who committed to the league in 2009. Agassi, who had played as an ambassador and league spokesman from 2002 to 2004, rejoined to play for King's Philadelphia Freedoms.

"First of all, it's been a few years since I've sort of been connected with the game in any direct kind of way, and that's been a little unsettling for me. I took time away when I retired to try to figure out how I can best engage with the game and do it in a way that made the most sense or where I could possibly have some more impact," said Agassi to reporters ahead of the season.

"And that has not been so easy with all of my responsibilities to sort of figure out. So before I got too far away, I wanted to sort of re-engage in certain respects and show an appreciation for the life and the platform that tennis has given me," he said, "and I thought no better way to sort of inject myself back into World TeamTennis."

He added, "I love what Billie and Ilana have built."

"I think it's a great asset to the game and I think an even greater asset to the tennis fans, taking this sport to the people is a great feeling," said Agassi. "The environment is unlike any other, and it's just a lot of fun. So I thought it would be maybe an easy way to sort of introduce my body again to it."

Asked about the WTT atmosphere, Agassi praised it. "I think it's a great format for both the players and the crowd. I mean, certainly it's a grinding season, so to take current, active players and stick them in another environment where they have to be out there for a number of hours and they can sort of pass the ball if you will, or sub or take their breaks," he said. "So it's a great environment for the players to engage, get aggressive and then be able to sort of unplug and allow somebody else to kick in."

Agassi continued, "And I think that versatility allows for a great experience for the crowd. You get to see singles, men's, women's, doubles, mixed; it's hard to get bored watching, that's for sure."

Kim Clijsters, meanwhile, made a career comeback thanks to WTT after a hiatus of over two years. "What attracts me the most about it is the way it's played," Clijsters said about playing in the league. "It's the motivation, the crowd, the input of the crowd, the team atmosphere, and everything. That's something that I really enjoy."

She added that she was looking forward to learning the WTT style of play. "It's going to be a challenge I think, trying that new format. I've never played with the scoring and the no-ad, no service lets and everything," said Clijsters. "It's going to be interesting for me as well because there are a lot of things in your mind where you just have to switch that button and forget about the routines that we always have had in tennis."

In another historic first for the league, legend Martina Navratilova, took part in her 20th WTT season by playing for the Boston Lobsters; this would be her last appearance in the league.

***

During Championship Weekend, the Washington Kastles advanced to their first league final with a 22-19 win against the New York Sportimes to set up a match against the Springfield Lasers.

In the championship match, it would be the Kastles to beat the Springfield Lasers in the final, winning 23-20 at home.

"In front of a breathless crowd, Olga Puchkova, the least likely hero in Kastles Stadium, saved three match points before winning a tiebreaker against the league's female MVP Vania King to win the 2009 Advanta WTT Championship," the match report began.

The Kastles were dominant from the start, winning the first three events before losing in women's doubles.

"Our success in this match and during our season was all about the team, and none of it would have been possible without Coach Murphy Jensen's leadership and the players pulling together to help get the most out of each other," said Mark Ein, the team's owner, after the match.

"We were thrilled to win the King Trophy and WTT Championship in front of the best fans in the league who lifted the team's play last night and so many times during the season," he added. "It was an incredible match that everyone will remember and that embodies all that is great about World TeamTennis."

The Kastles led by 13-9 going into halftime. "With all the pressure on them, Stubbs and Puchkova quickly seized the momentum against Vania King, 2009 WTT Female MVP and Huber, the world's top-ranked doubles player, and jumped out to a 3-1 lead," according to the franchise's archives. "However, the Lasers won the next four straight games to take the set 5-3. By cutting the Kastles' lead to two games at 16-14, the Lasers found themselves back into the match. The stage was set for a dramatic fifth event."

It continued: "On one end of the court was Vania King who had sparked the Lasers to victories so many times during the season with dramatic come-from-behind victories. On the other end was Olga Puchkova, the young, extremely talented, but sometimes nervous Russian who was faced with the seemingly impossible task of closing out the match with momentum in the Lasers' favor."

But Puchkova fought. "Down 4-2 in the set and 3-1 in the game, Puchkova clawed back from a three-championship point deficit by winning the next three points all on long rallies to win the game and get her and the Kastles back in the match," the report said. "In the next game, Puchkova held her serve for the first time in the match to tie the score at 4-4. In the deciding fifth set tiebreaker, Puchkova got off to a fast start and went on to win 5-2 to secure the set at 5-4 and earn the Kastles the championship."

"This whole season has been about one thing, bringing a championship trophy to Washington," said coach Murphy Jensen.

"Our team really came together and we could not have done it without the amazing Washington fans supporting us along the way," he added.

The Washington Kastles celebrate after Olga Puchkova wins women's singles and the Kastles claim their first World TeamTennis title in 2009. Photo: CameraworkUSA

***

The 2010 season marked the league's 35th anniversary, which featured top players including Andy Roddick, James Blake, Anna Kournikova, Maria Sharapova, Serena and Venus Williams, John McEnroe, and Lindsay Davenport, among other marquee players.

Martina Hingis, meanwhile, would be making a return to competitive play for the first time since 2007 by committing with the New York Buzz. In a conference call ahead of the season, Hingis discussed the comeback.

"I always loved tennis, so that never really stopped me from playing," she said. "I always liked the competition. I liked going out there and have a challenge and play some tennis. Just to have a little bit of that, that's what I'm looking for."

She added: "I hope that I can say the same thing when I am finished with TeamTennis. It is totally different from when you play tournaments that are mostly quiet. Here you have the music playing. You have the teammates rooting for you so I really like the team spirit. I have not played much, so it will be a great experience."

King and Kloss also spoke at length about the league in honor of the 35th season.

"Well, the reason we started it was we wanted tennis to be a team sport, a coed team sport and wanted something that would last two-and-a-half to three hours. Also, more importantly, to have equality, that there be an equal contribution by both genders on a level playing field," said King. "We thought it was very important for young people to see cooperation among the best players in the world, that everybody may have a chance to play for their home team some year."

She added, "I think it's going for 35 years because people like it. I think they like the coed. I think they like the fast pace. We have been the innovators of the sport."

King continued, "We've pushed the establishment to make it more fan friendly at many, many levels, playing let serves, substitutions, instant replay, on-court coaching, music between points, names on the back of players' shirts, letting fans keep the balls that are hit into the stands, multi-colored courts which is a branding thing we did in the '70s."

She said, "It's different, brings fans together and it's great to play for your community."

"I think one of the things that we've really always looked at is, how can we continue to innovate?" explained Kloss. "In sport, I think World TeamTennis is thought of as the innovator of the sport and the think tank. There's nothing wrong with trying something."

She added: "If it works great, you keep it. If you don't, that's okay. But to listen to the fans, to I think provide access to the sponsors and the media in a way that maybe other events can't. I think, you know, just continue to educate."

Kloss continued: "For us we find that we have a great product; we just really need communities to get out there and support it. Our season is pretty short. It's really a three-and-a-half week season with 73 matches, including regular-season playoffs and the championship match. It comes and goes very fast."

***

The 35th season saw the Kansas City Explorers advance to the finals for just the second time in their 18 years of existence, beating the Springfield Lasers 20-17 to advance.

"The Lasers started strong in the opening set as Rik de Voest broke Ricardo Mello's serve in the 8th game for a 5-3 win in the men's singles battle," according to the league's archives. "The Explorers' Jarmila Groth quickly took charge in women's singles and put the Explorers on top with a dominating 5-0 rout of Chani Scheepers in the second set."

In mixed doubles, both coaches interestingly elected to substitute their players mid-match to intensify the fight for the championship berth. One "substitution ignited the Lasers who won four consecutive points to tie the game score at 4-4," according to the match report. "During the tiebreaker, Explorers coach Brent Haygarth sent Mello in with Kansas City leading 3-1. Springfield won the next two points to bring it to 3-3." Ultimately, Jarmila Groth closed the mixed doubles set to grab the Explorers a 5-4 win and a 13-9 lead heading into halftime.

In women's doubles, Carly Gullickson and Scheepers nabbed a 5-2 win to get the Lasers within one point of the Explorers, ahead of the final set of men's doubles.

"Both teams held serve in men's doubles until the fifth game when the Explorers broke Damm's serve and moved ahead by two games in the overall match score, 18-16," according to the league archives. "Ricardo Mello and Sam Groth held on for a 5-3 win to send the Explorers to the finals on their home court."

In the other conference championship, the New York Sportimes beat the rain and their opponents, the Boston Lobsters, to get into the finals. The team won 22-17 in Overtime.

"The Sportimes were at the top of the Eastern Conference standings all season and continued their dominance tonight. But the Boston Lobsters, who defeated the defending WTT champion Washington Kastles last night, embodied WTT's most fundamental principles—every point counts and you are not out of contention until the last point is played," according to a match report. "With their team trailing 19-11 going into the fifth set, Eric Butorac and Raquel Kops-Jones put forth an impressive effort to take the final set 5-2 and force play to continue in Overtime."

Regardless, the Sportimes had a large seven-game lead thanks to their sharp play in the first four sets. Together, Robert Kendrick and Abigail Spears won to defeat their opponents.

"Before the match, I told the team, let's not argue calls, but focus on being mentally tough, because that is all you can control on court," said the Sportimes coach Chuck Adams. "One person dropping his or her head brings everyone down," but he said the team "did a good job staying positive tonight."

With the final set, the match took place in Kansas City pitting the Sportimes against the Explorers. "In the opening set, New York's Jesse Witten won three of four 3-all points to edge Mello in men's singles in the opening set of the 2010 WTT Finals," according to the league archives. "The husband and wife tandem of Jarka and Sam Groth pulled the Explorers even with the Sportimes after mixed doubles with a 5-3. Jarka Groth subbed in for Kveta Peschke with the Explorers trailing 1-2 and closed out her first game with an ace to even the score at 2-2."

But Kansas City broke Abigail Spears' serve in the game's seventh set to snatch a 4-3 lead and to win the set 5-3.

"Kansas City took the overall match lead at 10-9 in the third game of men's doubles, but the Sportimes countered by winning the next game to bring it even at 2-2 in the set, 10-10 in the match," according to the article. But the match proved to be a rollercoaster of sorts. After all, "The Sportimes took the lead when Sam Groth double-faulted in the fifth game of the set to give the Sportimes the 3-2 lead." Meanwhile, "Robert Kendrick and Witten kept the pressure on the Explorers with a 5-3 win to give the New York team a 13-11 halftime advantage."

Jarmila Groth, however, dug deep to take out Abigail Spears' serve and grab a 5-2 win to get the Explorers out front heading into the last set of the historic 35th season.

The Explorers' Jarmila and Kveta Peschke claimed a 5-3 win over the Sportimes' Ashley Harkleroad and Spears in the final set to end the season and get Kansas City their first King Trophy in their 18 years of action.

"Our crowd was awesome tonight and they helped us a lot through the whole three-week season," said Groth after the win, referring to the heavy chanting and electric atmosphere thanks to the team's fans. "They pushed us that extra step."

WTT FINALS 2006

Philadelphia Freedoms  21

Newport Beach Breakers 14

WTT FINALS 2007

Sacramento Capitals 24

New York Buzz 20

WTT FINALS 2008

New York Buzz 21

Kansas City Explorers 18

WTT FINALS 2009

| Washington Kastles | 23 |
| Springfield Lasers | 20 |

WTT FINALS 2010

| Kansas City Explorers | 21 |
| New York Sportimes | 18 |

Chapter Eight: Seasons Thirty-Six to Forty (2011-2015):

The Kastles Dominate

2011 TEAMS & PLAYERS:
EASTERN CONFERENCE:

Boston Lobsters:	James Blake, John Isner, Eric Butorac, Jan-Michael Gambill, CoCo Vandeweghe, Irina Falconi, Mashona Washington. COACH: Bud Schultz
New York Sportimes:	Martina Hingis, Robert Kendrick, John McEnroe, Katie O'Brien, Jesse Witten. COACH: Fritz Buehning
Philadelphia Freedoms:	Beatrice Capra, Jimmy Connors, Brendan Evans, Nathan Healey, Melanie Oudin, Lisa Raymond, Julia Cohen. COACH: Pascal Collard. ASST COACH: Josh Cohen
Washington Kastles:	Leander Paes, Sam Querrey, Bobby Reynolds, Arina Rodionova, Rennae Stubbs, Serena Williams, Venus Williams. COACH: Murphy Jensen

WESTERN CONFERENCE:

Kansas City Explorers:	Madison Brengle, Bob Bryan, Mike Bryan, Alex Kuznetsov, Ricardo Mello, Kveta Peschke. COACH: Brent Haygarth
Newport Beach Breakers:	Lester Cook, Taylor Dent, Anne Keothavong, Marie-Eve Pelletier, Travis Rettenmaier, Pete Sampras. COACH: Trevor Kronemann
Sacramento Capitals:	Mardy Fish, Vania King, Mark Knowles, Yasmin Schnack, Dusan Vemic, Christina Fusano. COACH: Wayne Bryan
Springfield Lasers:	Rik de Voest, Paul Hanley, Carly Gullickson, Raven Klaasen, Lilia Osterloh. COACH: John-Laffnie de Jager. ASST COACH: Martin Damm
St. Louis Aces:	Roman Borvanov, Lindsay Davenport, Liezel Huber, Mark Philippoussis, Jean-Julien Rojer. COACH: Rick Leach
WTT FINALS (in Charleston, S.C.):	Washington Kastles def. St. Louis Aces 23-19

2012 TEAMS & PLAYERS:

EASTERN CONFERENCE:

Boston Lobsters:	Andre Agassi, John Isner, Eric Butorac, Irina Falconi, Jan-Michael Gambill, Robby Ginepri, Carly Gullickson-Eagle. COACH: Bud Schultz
New York Sportimes:	Martina Hingis, Robert Kendrick, John McEnroe, Ashley Harkleroad, Jesse Witten, Kveta Peschke, Abigail Spears. COACH: Chuck Adams
Philadelphia Freedoms:	James Blake, Mark Philippoussis, Luka Gregorc, Jordan Kerr, Karolina Pliskova, Kristyna Pliskova. COACH: Josh Cohen
Washington Kastles:	Venus Williams, Raquel Kops-Jones, Leander Paes, Bobby Reynolds, Anastasia Rodionova, Arina Rodionova, Edina Gallovits-Hall, Treat Huey. COACH: Murphy Jensen

WESTERN CONFERENCE:

Kansas City Explorers:	Tetiana Luzhanska, Bob Bryan, Mike Bryan, Nick Monroe, Chanel Simmonds, Aisam-Ul-Haq Qureshi. COACH: Brent Haygarth
Orange County Breakers:	Lindsay Davenport, Anna-Lena Groenefeld, Travis Parrot, John-Patrick Smith, Jana Juricova. COACH: Trevor Kronemann
Sacramento Capitals:	Mardy Fish, Sam Querrey, Kevin Anderson, Mark Knowles, Asia Muhammad, Yasmin Schnack, Ryan Sweeting, CoCo Vandeweghe, Vania King, Alex Kuznetsov. COACH: Wayne Bryan
Springfield Lasers:	Timea Babos, Devin Britton, Maria Sanchez, Amir Weintraub, Liga Dekmeijere. COACH: John-Laffnie de Jager.
WTT FINALS *(in Charleston, S.C.)*:	Washington Kastles def. Sacramento Capitals 20-19

2013 TEAMS & PLAYERS:

EASTERN CONFERENCE:

Boston Lobsters:	Eric Butorac, Jill Craybas, Amir Weintraub, Katalin Marosi, Mark Philippoussis. COACH: Bud Schultz
New York Sportimes:	Anna-Lena Groenefeld, Robert Kendrick, John McEnroe, Kveta Peschke, Jesse Witten. COACH: Claude Okin
Philadelphia Freedoms:	Vicky Duval, Sam Groth, Liezel Huber, Jordan Kerr, Sachia Vickery. COACH: Josh Cohen
Washington Kastles:	Kevin Anderson, Martina Hingis, Frederik Nielsen, Leander Paes, Bobby Reynolds, Anastasia Rodionova. COACH: Murphy Jensen

WESTERN CONFERENCE:

Texas Wild	Alex Bogomolov Jr., Eugenie Bouchard, Bob Bryan, Mike Bryan, Darija Jurak, Aisam Qureshi. COACH: Brent Haygarth
Orange County Breakers:	Maria Elena Camerin, Liga Dekmeijere, Treat Huey, Steve Johnson, CoCo Vandeweghe. COACH: Trevor Kronemann

Sacramento Capitals:	Mardy Fish, Olga Govortsova, Mark Knowles,, Megan Moulton-Levy, Sam Querrey, Ryan Sweeting, Taylor Townsend.
	COACH: Wayne Bryan
Springfield Lasers:	Springfield Lasers: Rik de Voest, Vania King, Alisa Kleybanova, Andy Roddick, Jean-Julien Rojer.
	COACH: John-Laffnie de Jager
Mylan WTT FINALS (in Washington D.C.):	WASHINGTON KASTLES def. Springfield Lasers 25-12

2014 TEAMS & PLAYERS:
EASTERN CONFERENCE:

Boston Lobsters:	Eric Butorac, James Cerretani, Sharon Fichman, John Isner, Megan Moulton-Levy, Rik de Voest, Caitlin Whoriskey.
	COACH: Robert Greene
Philadelphia Freedoms:	Frank Dancevic, Liezel Huber, Marcelo Melo, Taylor Townsend.
	COACH: Josh Cohen
Washington Kastles:	Martina Hingis, Leander Paes, Bobby Reynolds, Anastasia Rodionova, Venus Williams. COACH: Murphy Jensen

WESTERN CONFERENCE:

Austin Aces:	Marion Bartoli, Eva Hrdinova, Treat Huey, Andy Roddick, Vera Zvonareva.
	COACH: Rick Leach
San Diego Aviators:	Bob Bryan, Mike Bryan, Somdev Devvarman, Daniela Hantuchova, Raven Klaasen, Kveta Peschke. COACH: David Macpherson
Springfield Lasers:	Liga Dekmeijere, Olga Govortsova, Ross Hutchins, Raquel Kops-Jones, Michael Russell, Abigail Spears. COACH: John-Laffnie de Jager.
Texas Wild	Alex Bogomolov Jr., Anabel Medina Garrigues, Darija Jurak, Aisam Qureshi. COACH: Brent Haygarth
Mylan WTT FINALS (in Springfield, Mo.):	WASHINGTON KASTLES def. Springfield Lasers 25-13

2015 TEAMS & PLAYERS:
EASTERN CONFERENCE:

| Boston Lobsters: | Irina Falconi, Scott Lipsky, Maria Sanchez, Arantxa Parra Santonja, Alex Kuznetsov, Tim Smyczek. COACH: Jan-Michael Gambill |
| Philadelphia Freedoms: | Robby Ginepri, Marcelo Melo, Asia Muhammad, Abigail Spears, Taylor Townsend, CoCo Vandeweghe. COACH: Josh Cohen |

Washington Kastles:	Madison Brengle, Martina Hingis, Denis Kudla, Leander Paes, Sam Querrey, Anastasia Rodionova, Venus Williams. COACH: Murphy Jensen

WESTERN CONFERENCE:

Austin Aces:	Teymuraz Gabashvili, Nicole Gibbs, Jarmere Jenkins, Alla Kudryavtseva, Elina Svitolina. COACH: Rick Leach
California Dream	Bob Bryan, Mike Bryan, Jarka Gajdosova, Anabel Medina Garrigues, Tennys Sandgren, Neal Skupski. COACH: David Macpherson
San Diego Aviators:	Taylor Fritz, Darija Jurak, Madison Keys, Raven Klaasen, Chani Scheepers. COACH: John Lloyd
Springfield Lasers:	Andre Begemann, Anna-Lena Groenefeld, John Isner, Alison Riske, Michael Russell, Sachia Vickery, Varvara Lepchenko. COACH: John-Laffnie de Jager.
Mylan WTT FINALS *(in Washington, DC):*	WASHINGTON KASTLES def. Austin Aces 24-18

The Washington Kastles may have won one title from 2006 to 2010, but they were about to become the biggest force in the league with teamwork that took them to even greater heights. In fact, the Kastles would even go on to claim two consecutive seasons without dropping a match.

With the 36th season kicking off, Venus Williams helped the Kastles to a victory over the Kansas City Explorers on July 5 in a tight 21-18 match that was forced into Overtime. Although she ended up losing to compatriot Christina McHale in a close 5-4 loss that day, she took the time to reflect on her experience with WTT after the match.

She remembered playing in a World TeamTennis clinic in the 1980s and said that's when she first identified her passion for the sport and how good she could become, according to *The Washington Post*. She also met Billie Jean King for the first time after her father had won a raffle.

"I really wanted to impress her," Williams said in an interview after her team's win. "I thought I was great. Let's hope I was, but I thought I was."

Serena Williams helped the Washington Kastles claim titles in 2009 and 2011. Photo: CameraworkUSA

"It was just an unbelievable day," Williams said. "We had pizza. It really wasn't until decades later that I realized that was [World] TeamTennis and that was one of the clinics. And it's just amazing how it becomes full circle. Hopefully one day, [the kids will] be professionals and say 'I remember…..'"

"To have her play for the Washington Kastles, I mean, c'mon, look at that serve, look at that forehand, and look how she embraces the city of DC," said the Kastles Coach Murphy Jensen in an interview about his player's prowess on-court. Williams "more than helps. We're talking about the biggest striker in the history of the women's game."

As the season wore on for the Kastles, it became quickly apparent that something special was taking place, as they continually won tight matches. Near the end of the season, for instance, the Kastles rolled to an 11-0 victory after a particularly powerful display against the Sacramento Capitals, the winningest team in the league's history, by 25-14.

"Rookie Arina Rodionova routed world No. 90 Vania King 5-0 in women's singles to give the Washington Kastles an insurmountable lead on their way to a 25-14 victory over the Sacramento Capitals Monday night in front of another sellout crowd at Kastles Stadium at The Wharf," according to the team's archives.

The Kastles would be just three wins away from the 1994 Newport Beach Dukes' perfect regular season, the only time something like that had happened.

"With its win Monday, Washington ensured that it will finish with the league's best record, which makes the Kastles the No. 1 overall seed at WTT Championship Weekend in Charleston, South Carolina," according to the match report.

"After one-game wins in its previous three home matches, Washington swept all five sets against Sacramento," it continued.

Rodionova proved to be a standout during the match, striking blistering forehands against King. "'Hot Rod' had to wait her turn, however, because the match began with a mixed doubles set featuring four Grand Slam doubles champions," the report continued, "With a timely return in a tiebreak, the WTT's No. 1 mixed doubles team of Rennae Stubbs and Leander Paes won their sixth straight set together with a 5-4(3) victory over King and Mark Knowles."

Fast forward to men's doubles, and the Kastles nabbed a 15-10 lead as the team continued to break their opponent's' serve. Rodionova continued to be on a tear as she helped her team to a 20-10 lead just minutes later after women's singles.

"The Kastles' rookie was rewarded afterward when Paes shined her tennis shoes with a towel, much to the delight of the sold-out crowd," according to the match report.

The final event in men's singles also went the Kastles' way, with Bobby Reynolds striking aces to close out the event, for yet another win for the Washington franchise.

Just days later that form continued when the Kastles ended the regular season by taking out the Philadelphia Freedoms 25-11. In doing so, they became just the second WTT team (after the Dukes in 1994) to grab a perfect regular season.

The Kastles also became the top seed in the Eastern Conference Championship. "Leander Paes, who was announced as the 2011 WTT Male MVP prior to the match, partnered with Rennae Stubbs to power past Boston's Eric Butorac and Mashona Washington, 5-2, in the opening set," in the conference final, according to the league's archives.

"That opening match set the tone for the rest of the first half as Stubbs and Arina Rodionova dominated Washington and her partner Irina Falconi in women's doubles 5-1. The Kastles cruised to a 15-5 halftime lead after Paes and Bobby Reynolds defeated Butorac and Jan-Michael Gambill in men's doubles, 5-2," it continued.

But Boston did get a win when Irina Falconi edged a win over WTT's Female Rookie of the Year Arina Rodionova by 5-4 in the set.

While Jan-Michael Gambill won men's singles 5-3 to send the match into Overtime, it would be Bobby Reynolds to close out Washington's 15th consecutive victory by winning the first game in extended, which would halt the momentum swing from Gambill. That gave the Kastles a 23-15 win.

"The win gives 2011 Coach of the Year Murphy Jensen and his squad a shot at making WTT history on Sunday's final. No team in WTT history has ever gone undefeated throughout the entire regular and post-season," according to the archives.

In the other conference championship, the St. Louis Aces played against the Sacramento Capitals for a spot in the final. "Dusan Vemic gave Sacramento an early lead with a 5-3 singles victory over St. Louis' Roman Borvanov," according to a match report. "St. Louis took over the lead when Tamira Paszek ran past Vania King of Sacramento in women's singles 5-1."

By halftime, the score became tied at 11-all when the Capitals men's doubles team won 5-3.

"King and Yasmin Schnack upset 2011 WTT Female MVP Liezel Huber and Paszek in women's doubles in a tight 5-4 set, giving the Capitals a one-point lead, 16-15, heading into the final set of mixed doubles," the report continued.

Huber and Rojer of the Aces secured the only service break in the final set to grab a 5-3 victory over Knowles and King as the American doubles specialist saw her shot sail wide on match point.

"Every point, every game counts," said Huber about her team's victory. "I wanted to win so bad for my team and St. Louis tonight."

Huber looked ahead to the championship match against the Kastles, too. "They are a great team but we start from scratch tomorrow," she said. "We have nothing to lose."

On a day flushed out by rain on and off, the Kastles took on the Aces in Charleston, South Carolina, for the match to decide the winner of that year's King Trophy.

"Slowed by the first rain delay shortly after the 5 p.m. match start time, it took more than three hours for St. Louis to win the opening set of mixed doubles, 5-3," according to a match report. "The Aces, led by Jean-Julien Rojer and 2011 Female MVP Liezel Huber, won 72% of their first service points in a tight battle with Male MVP Leander Paes and Rennae Stubbs."

In women's doubles, Stubbs and Rodionova blanked Huber and Tamira Paszek, 5-0, to secure an 8-5 lead for the Kastles after the second set. In men's doubles, the Kastles claimed a 5-2 win over Rojer and Roman Borvanov.

"Rodionova, who was named MVP of the WTT Finals, took control in women's singles and edged Paszek to push the Kastles lead to seven games heading into the final set," the report added. Although "St. Louis staged an impressive rally in men's singles with Borvanov holding off Reynolds 5-4 to send the match into Overtime, Borvanov won the first three games in Overtime to close the gap to 22-19," and it was Bobby Reynolds who held serve to close out the historic victory after 1 a.m. in the morning.

The win meant the Kastles became the first team in WTT history to claim a perfect 16-0 record in the league's 36 seasons.

***

Highlight #8: The Magic behind the Kastles

Every good team needs a strong leader, and Mark Ein, the owner of the Washington Kastles, is that person. Ein's team has dominated the league in its prime, including collecting six titles in seven seasons.

Ein, the CEO of Venturehouse Group, has always had a passion for tennis. As an adult, he jumped at the chance to own a tennis franchise in the country's capital, Washington, D.C. After speaking with King and Kloss in 2007 at the WTT suite at the US Open, Ein decided to go through with buying the team and kicking off a franchise of his own.

Ein said he began with a mission: "It really was all about unity and has nothing to do with winning championships or winning matches or winning streaks," he said. "It all really has to do with let's try to do something great for our community."

The Washington Kastles won the King Trophy in 2014. Pictured (front row): Anastasia Rodionova, Martina Hingis, Leander Paes, Bobby Reynolds; (back row) WTT CEO/Commissioner Ilana Kloss, owner Mark Ein, coach Murphy Jensen and WTT co-founder Billie Jean King. Photo: CameraworkUSA

He added: "I think this having sort of that community focus and sort of a notion that this is about something bigger than tennis, bigger than any of the players. I think that's one of the reason they've honestly been inspired to just rise to these incredible levels and play so well."

Ein has also praised the efforts of King and the founders for beginning the league. "It's men and women on the same team working together towards the common goal," he said. "It's a philosophy. It's great and inspiring … it's so incredible."

He continued: "But, what you really find when you interview the players who play World TeamTennis is that they never feel more pressure and they never feel more intensity, than when they're playing World TeamTennis."

To that effect, Ilana Kloss praised Ein's determination and leadership over the course of his Kastles' success. "It's all about the teams. You need a great leader and simply Mark has been a great leader," she said. "But, I think, he's built a team of people that includes the players. They all are very important."

She also praised Ein's decision to select Murphy Jensen, a former WTT star, for his team's coach. "Obviously, Murphy played World TeamTennis. He's got good energy. The great thing about World TeamTennis it also allows a lot of players to have an extended career," she said. "So, you might just stop playing, but you can still coach. You can still be involved. You can work for the team. I think, you know, it's been a win-win. It's been great for Murphy's career and at the same time it's been good for the team."

Ein continued discussing King's vision and how it's felt for him to add to her legacy as the Kastles' owner by promoting equality. "I think that's also part of something that Billie innately understands that whether it's the players, the fans or the community, that playing for something for something bigger than yourself is really an inspiration," he said. "That's what World TeamTennis represents."

"This undefeated championship season is a dream come true for our franchise and for our incredible players, coach, fans and the entire community without whom none of this could have been possible," said owner Mark Ein after the win. "It's been a perfect year in every respect for the Washington Kastles organization."

He added, "This unprecedented result shows the power of teamwork, both on and off the court, as these players came together to support, love and help one another so that the whole was so much more than the sum of the individual pieces."

"This is one of the greatest moments in all of our tennis careers," said coach Murphy Jensen after the match. "Being a part of the incredible Kastles organization, representing their amazing fans and working together with these players to do something that hasn't been done in the 36 years of WTT history is something all of us will cherish for the rest of our lives."

***

In 2012, the league celebrated its 37th season as well as the 40th anniversary of Title IX, the legislation that promotes equality for women and men in education programs.

"No person in the United States shall, on the basis of sex, be excluded from participation in, be denied the benefits of, or be subjected to discrimination under any education program or activity receiving Federal financial assistance," reads the legislation, which King fought for throughout her career and with the help of the "Battle of the Sexes" match, in which she defeated Bobby Riggs in front of millions.

"When I was 11 years old, I played tennis for the first time. As a young girl, I quickly realized that the sport was very uniform with little to no diversity in everything from clothing to class, to race and gender," she wrote in an essay for *USA Today*.

"At 12 years old, I knew two things about my quest in life: I wanted to be the No. 1 tennis player in the world, and I wanted to use my success to change the face of our society to grant equal rights and opportunities for both men and women."

King added: "In 1974, only two years after Title IX was enacted, I founded the Women's Sports Foundation, an organization dedicated to advancing the lives of females through sports and physical activity."

King wrote that Title IX will keep more women participating in sport every year, too. "Just as we do for our sons, we as a nation must support our daughters' sports participation. Keeping girls in the game has a profound positive impact on their physical and emotional health, academic careers and financial success as adults," she explained. "Many of these women will perfect the skills they learn and become elite athletes and coaches, strong business women, scientists, lawyers, doctors, educators and other valuable members of society."

King continued: "That is the beauty of Title IX—then and now—it gives young women the tools to become whatever they want to be in life. Help keep her in the game."

***

Along with the historic significance of WTT celebrating Title IX's anniversary, the league was in the midst of one team making history in its own right: the Washington Kastles' winning streak was still very much alive.

Indeed, the Kastles wouldn't relent in their play to start the season. As the season started, the Washington franchise won their 17th straight match in a 22-18 victory over the Orange County Breakers.

"Leading the way for Washington in the first World TeamTennis match of 2012 was two-time league MVP Leander Paes, who teamed with Anastasia Rodionova to win mixed doubles 5-1 before partnering Bobby Reynolds to a 5-3 win in men's doubles," according to a match report on the results.

"It was a remarkable performance from Paes, who arrived in California just before the match after flying over 12 hours from London. The two-time WTT Male MVP played in the Wimbledon mixed doubles final on Sunday and competed in each of the last seven days of that tournament," it continued. "By the time the last ball was played in Orange County at 12:30 am DC time, it had been almost 24 hours since Paes' wake-up call in London one day earlier."

But Paes proved pivotal to the match as his wins "propelled Washington to a 17-14 lead entering the fifth set, which the Kastles' closer Reynolds clinched 5-4 in men's singles." Reynolds, meanwhile, saved three set points against John-Patrick Smith before defeating him and the Breakers "with an ace out wide on the Kastles' first match point."

As the season wore on and players from the Kastles, such as Leander Paes, and others flew to London to play in the Summer Olympics, the franchise from Washington continued to win.

In fact, they became the first U.S. pro sports team to complete back-to-back seasons without losing. At the end of July, the Kastles advanced to their second straight Eastern Conference Championship by beating the Springfield Lasers 25-14 to claim consecutive win No. 30.

"The Kastles are now only three matches away from equaling the longest winning streak in major U.S. pro sports history, set by the 1971-72 Los Angeles Lakers. Since losing to the Boston Lobsters on July 22, 2010, Washington has finished consecutive regular seasons 14-0 and won a pair of matches during the 2011 WTT Finals Weekend to capture the WTT Championship for the second time in three years," according to a write-up by Kastles' staff writer Joshua Rey.

"It gives me goosebumps and brings me to tears to think of the experience that we've had," said coach Murphy Jensen.

In the Conference Championships Weekend, which took place in South Carolina in September, the Sacramento Capitals advanced to the finals by beating the Orange County Breakers.

The Capitals would vie for a seventh WTT title with a victory in the championship match, a league best.

Against the Breakers, "Sacramento jumped out to an early lead with a first set win in men's singles," according to a match report. "Kevin Anderson overpowered the Breakers' John-Patrick Smith 5-3. Anderson started mixed doubles and won the first game on the South African's big serve before Caps coach Wayne Bryan brought in doubles great Mark Knowles to join CoCo Vandeweghe." It continued, "Knowles was spectacular, hitting winners and leading the Caps to a 5-4 set win with Yasmin Schnack, who replaced Vandeweghe at 2-2."

The team from Sacramento led 15-8 going into halftime as Anderson and Knowles outplayed Smith and Travis Parrott in men's doubles, 5-1. In women's singles, CoCo Vandeweghe beat the Breakers' Jana Juricova 5-4 in women's singles to get her team an eight-game lead with just one set left in the match.

Schnack and Asia Muhammad ended the match in Sacramento's favor by winning women's doubles 5-3 over Groenefeld and Juricova to advance to the championship match.

In the second conference match, the Kastles kept their streak alive by beating the New York Sportimes to set up a final with the Capitals and a shot at another title.

With the final set and history on the line for both teams, it would be Venus Williams to make the difference for her Washington team. In fact, she led her team to the title.

Sacramento got off to an early start when Kevin Anderson took out Bobby Reynolds in the first set by 5-3.

But Washington turned the tables in women's doubles with the help of Williams, who helped grab a 5-1 set win.

"Men's doubles was highlighted by brilliant shot-making by the Kastles' Leander Paes, but it was the Caps that broke Paes' serve for a 2-1 lead. Anderson pushed the lead to 4-2 on his serve and broke Paes' serve for a second time to take the set 5-2 and lead 11-10 at halftime," according to a match report.

In mixed doubles, Washington ended up winning the set in a tight 5-4 win after a 9-point tiebreak. That made the score going into the final set of women's singles tied at 15-all.

"Williams edged CoCo Vandeweghe 5-4 in women's singles to give the Kastles their third title in the past four seasons," according to the article. "Although Williams was part of championship teams in Philadelphia and Washington, this was the first time she had played in the championship match."

"I had to come out on fire today," said Williams about the victory. "Knowing I had to play for my team was motivating."

The win also meant the Kastles had collected 32 wins, just one shy of the longest streak in U.S. pro sports history, the record for which was held by the NBA's Lakers in 1971 to 1972.

***

The 38th season of WTT started with all eyes on the Washington Kastles to see if they could keep their momentum going as well as the 32-match winning streak. They'd win their 33rd match to tie the Lakers' record.

Soon after, the Kastles claimed win No. 34, too, to become the winningest team in United States major pro sports teams history.

"With tonight's 25-12 victory over the Boston Lobsters in Washington, DC, the Kastles extended their win streak to 34 consecutive matches, breaking the previous record they shared with the NBA's 1971-72 Los Angeles Lakers," according to the WTT archives.

"The Kastles won the 2011 and 2012 Mylan World TeamTennis titles with two 16-0 seasons. The last time the Kastles lost a match was on Thursday, July 22, 2010, when the Boston Lobsters defeated the Kastles, 24-15, in Overtime in the final match of the 2010 regular season. The loss propelled Boston into the 2010 playoffs and kept the Kastles out of post-season action," it added.

The Kastles started strongly to help set up the win as Kevin Anderson got a 5-2 win over Boston's Amir Weintraub. "The Kastles continued to roll in women's doubles, with Martina Hingis and Anastasia Rodionova posting a 5-3 win over Jill Craybas and Katalin Marosi. The Kastles built up a 15-8 halftime lead," the match report continued.

"Hingis was too much for Craybas in women's singles, winning 5-2," the article added. "They closed out their historic win with Paes and Bobby Reynolds topping Weintraub and Butorac 5-2 in the final set."

Jeanie Buss, president of the Los Angeles Lakers, was a World TeamTennis executive in the 1980s for the Los Angeles Strings.

She congratulated the Kastles on their achievements and for breaking the record set by her team. "Winning 33 consecutive games was an amazing accomplishment by our 1971-72 Lakers team, as evidenced by the fact that no other team has come close to reaching it for over 40 years now," she said in a statement.

"On behalf of the Buss family and the Lakers family, I want to congratulate the Washington Kastles, their players, and our good friends Billie Jean King and Ilana Kloss on this milestone accomplishment of theirs," she added.

But the Kastles' streak wouldn't go any further. In fact, in their very next match, the Kastles lost to the Texas Wild.

"The Wild ended the Kastles' amazing run of 34 consecutive wins with a 23-18 victory on Wednesday evening at Wild Stadium at the Four Seasons Resort & Club Dallas at Las Colinas in Irving, Texas," according to the WTT archives. "One night earlier, the Kastles set the mark for the longest win streak in major U.S. pro sports history in Washington, D.C. Before tonight, the last time the Kastles lost a match was July 22, 2010."

Although the Kastles began with a strong start in men's doubles with Leander Paes in tow, the Wild claimed the next two sets in women's doubles and men's singles for a 13-12 lead at halftime.

"A close battle in mixed doubles saw Qureshi and Darija Jurak emerge as the victors over Paes and Anastasia Rodionova after rallying from 2-4 in the tiebreaker to win the set and take an 18-16 lead into the final event," according to the match report.

"The women would decide the final results as women's singles closed out the night. Eugenie Bouchard was too tough, outlasting Rodionova 5-2 to give the Wild the victory, their second in three matches this season," it continued.

Despite the loss, however, the Kastles were too good over the rest of the season. After all, the team advanced to the Eastern Conference Championships for the third straight year.

The team took out the Boston Lobsters in a 25-12 victory to get a step closer to becoming just the second team after the Sacramento Capitals to win three consecutive league titles.

After getting defeated back-to-back earlier in the season, the Kastles claimed a run of 11 straight wins heading into the final.

"Taking the court against the Lobsters for the second day in a row, the Kastles never trailed in the match. The Kastles made their first move in the opening set of mixed doubles, as newly crowned Mylan WTT Female MVP Martina Hingis and team captain Leander Paes broke Eric Butorac's serve for a 4-2 lead and closed out the American and Katalin Marosi in the ensuing game," according to a match report.

It added: "Hingis stayed on court to partner Anastasia Rodionova to a commanding 5-1 victory against Marosi and Jill Craybas in women's doubles."

Men's doubles also went the way of the Kastles as the team took a 15-5 lead going into halftime.

In women's singles, Hingis beat Craybas 5-2, while, in men's singles, Reynolds beat Weintraub in Overtime to close the match.

"It was a great match," said Hingis after the win. "I started out with Leander, who is a great mixed partner and we kept our winning streak going. In doubles with Anastasia, we did much better than last night [against the Lobsters]. Our team tried to get the same flow going as yesterday, as we knew we had to be ready, and we were."

The Kastles' opponents in the championship match? The Springfield Lasers, who annihilated the Texas Wild by 25-9 in the Western Conference Championship.

The Lasers had the home court advantage to begin the match at the Mediacom Stadium at Cooper Tennis Complex. The team grabbed a 5-3 lead to start as Rik de Voest beat Texas' Alex Bogomolov Jr. 5-3.

"Before the match, league officials announced that Jean-Julien Rojer was the 2013 Mylan WTT Male MVP while teammate Alisa Kleybanova was named Mylan WTT Female Rookie," according to the match write-up. "In the second set, Rojer and Kleybanova showed off the skills that earned them those accolades with a 5-3 win in mixed doubles over Bogomolov and Eugenie Bouchard."

The team led 15-7 heading into halftime, thanks to Rojer and de Voest beating Bogomolov and Aisam Qureshi 5-1 in men's doubles. Kleybanova got the same score in women's singles against Canada's Eugenie Bouchard.

The match ended when Kleybanova and Vania King claimed a 5-1 win in women's doubles to get the overall 25-9 victory for Springfield.

"This win means a lot. I can't say enough about this team and the way they produced," said coach John-Laffnie de Jager. "The Rookie of the Year and the Most Valuable Player showed why they got their prizes."

"We're not just happy to be in the finals, we want to win it. We have an unbelievable team. We help each other and the results show it," said Kleybanova after her team's victory.

Meanwhile, Andy Roddick would join his Lasers on the court for the finals against the Kastles. "Andy brings experience and a great presence to our team," said de Jager. "He's part of this team, he cares for the team and he wants the team to win."

***

In the finals, play was delayed by two hours thanks to the rain. And the Kastles made a switch, beginning with Bobby Reynolds in men's singles, despite him typically playing last to clinch wins. "Reynolds consistently applied pressure in de Voest's service games and after missing out on four break points in the second game, broke the South African twice to defeat de Voest 5-1 for the second time this season," according to a match report.

"The second set saw Hingis take the court for the first time, alongside Rodionova against Vania King and Mylan WTT Female Rookie of the Year Alisa Kleybanova in women's doubles. Up 3-2, the Lasers missed out on two break point chances, and Hingis and Rodionova went on to claim the final three games to extend the Kastles' lead," it continued.

"I am a first time Kastle. It's a great team," Hingis said afterward. "I love everyone and I hope I can play here again next year!"

Washington continued its momentum as the match wore on with a win in men's doubles to set up a 15-6 lead going into halftime.

Hingis and Kleybanova played in women's singles with the Swiss using her variety to beat the Russian 5-2.

With the match coming down to mixed doubles, Hingis and Paes grabbed a 4-2 lead against Kleybanova and Andy Roddick. Although the Lasers fought to force a tiebreaker, Paes clinched the title for the Kastles with a forehand return winner.

Andy Roddick, pictured with Billie Jean King, joined the WTT Ownership Group in 2013 along with Venus Williams. Photo: CameraworkUSA

The victory extended the Kastles' record to three straight titles and four overall. According to the league's archives: "Washington is the first franchise to take all five sets in the Mylan WTT Finals since the league switched to a first to five games format in 1999. It also marked the largest margin of victory by a winning team in the title match during this time, breaking the previous mark held by the Capitals in 2002 when they beat the New York Buzz by eight games."

"To come out and play in front of [the fans] here is amazing," said Reynolds after his team claimed the King Trophy. "I want to also thank my great team. We have so much support on the bench. This is a team effort."

***

The 38th season of WTT began with a big change for the league: a new title sponsor. Pharmaceuticals giant Mylan announced a partnership together, renaming it Mylan World TeamTennis in the process. "Mylan chose to partner with WTT due to our organizations' shared commitment to helping people around the world overcome barriers to access," according to CEO Heather Bresch. "For WTT, access means making sure everyone has the opportunity to participate on a team, preparing people—regardless of age, gender or race—to compete both in sports and in life. For Mylan, access is our purpose."

"Mylan and WTT share the same ideal of access and opportunity for everyone," said Kloss. "We are excited to partner with a global company like Mylan, and we will work together to elevate our respective brands and create greater opportunities for access both in the U.S. and international markets."

For its 39th season, WTT added two new franchises, including one in Austin, Texas, called the Aces, which saw Andy Roddick participate after he became part of the ownership group for the league in 2013.

Roddick, who played for the league first in 2000 as a member of the Idaho Sneakers, spoke about having a team in his hometown and playing for it.

"I have always been excited to be a part of Mylan WTT. I would have never thought back in 2000 when I was a WTT rookie in Boise, Idaho that I'd be a part of bringing a franchise to my hometown of Austin, Texas," he said. "I couldn't be luckier to be a part of this team."

Victoria Azarenka, the top-ranked player at the time, also spoke about her decision to sign up to play for the Philadelphia Freedoms. She first played for the league in 2006 as a teenager when she played for the Springfield Lasers and was named the Mylan WTT Female Rookie of the Year.

"I've always loved Mylan WTT as it is so enjoyable yet competitive. I have to say that I also love playing on the colored court," she said.

"To play for BJK's team means so much to me. If it wasn't for her, women's tennis wouldn't have what it has right now. I'm just really honored to be playing for her team," added Azarenka.

As the season wore on, the Washington Kastles would go on another winning streak, claiming 18 match wins in a row dating back to the prior season. Although they would go on to lose to the San Diego Aviators, the team still had six wins to just one loss for the season and a strong claim to a fourth consecutive King Trophy.

The Kastles would make that dream an even greater chance at becoming a reality by claiming the Eastern Conference Championship against the Philadelphia Freedoms.

"Bobby Reynolds led off for the Kastles in men's singles, winning the first 10 points before Frank Dancevic dug in for the Freedoms. It was a fierce battle, but Reynolds drew on his home fans to push ahead for a 5-3 win," according to a match report.

In women's singles, Martina Hingis lost to Taylor Townsend 5-2 to lose the lead to the Freedoms 8-7.

Taylor Townsend played her first season of World TeamTennis in 2013. Photo: CameraworkUSA

But Hingis played mixed doubles with Leander Paes, and they came out on top against Liezel Huber and Marcelo Melo by winning 5-2 to grab a 12-10 lead at halftime.

"Huber and Townsend hoped to keep the Freedoms close in women's doubles versus Hingis and Anastasia Rodionova. In the first game, Huber was struck in the back of the head by a Townsend forehand," according to a match report. "The Freedoms would win the game, but a few points later, Huber was unable to continue. It was later determined that she suffered a concussion."

Then something unorthodox happened: "Townsend continued to play one-on-two and held a game point on her serve, but Hingis and Rodionova finished off a 5-1 win."

In men's doubles, Dancevic and Melo defeated Reynolds and Paes 5-3 in men's doubles to make it to Overtime.

"Reynolds, who announced he was retiring from professional tennis after the Mylan WTT season, fittingly sealed the victory for Washington" for a spot in the finals by a final score of 21-16.

In the Western Conference Championship, Springfield's Michael Russell beat San Diego's Somdev Devvarman in the opening set 5-4.

Springfield held opportunities in women's doubles as Liga Dekmeijere-Thomas and Olga Govortsova got the set even from 4-1 down to 4-4. But the Aviators converted a third set point to get San Diego a 5-4 win and to even the score at 9-9 overall.

"In an entertaining set full of highlight worthy action, Bob Bryan and Kveta Peschke were too strong for Govortsova and Ross Hutchins. The Lasers broke Peschke's serve to go up 2-1, but the Aviators broke back on Govortsova's serve to even up the set at 2-2. Peschke and Bryan pulled away 5-3 to give San Diego a 14-12 halftime lead," according to a match report.

In women's singles, Govortsova beat Hantuchova 5-0 so that the Lasers led 17-14 going into the final set. Russell and Hutchins secured a 5-3 win over Bob and Mike Bryan in men's doubles to advance to the finals against the Kastles.

Bob Bryan and brother Mike have been part of championship seasons with Newport Beach and the Kansas City Explorers. Photo: CameraworkUSA

The finals saw the Kastles in charge from the opening set as Bobby Reynolds, who was playing in his final professional singles match, beat Springfield's Michael Russell 5-4.

"We knew Springfield was solid. I had some trouble with Mike the first two times we played," said Reynolds after the match. "I knew I needed to get to five. That was my goal today. I got down a break, but I was able to fight back. One thing about Mylan WTT is that you have to win those 3-all points and if you do, it's in your favor in the end."

In women's singles, Springfield's Olga Govortsova took a 2-0 lead after breaking serve when Hingis served a double fault. "Surprisingly, Govortsova returned the favor in the next game with a double fault to give Hingis a service break. Hingis got back on track serving an ace to even up the set at 2-2," a match report stated.

"She reeled off five straight games and converted four 3-all game points for a 5-2 victory that set the course for the afternoon," it continued.

"It was a great day here in Springfield for me, obviously with getting the Finals MVP," Hingis said in an interview after the match. "I don't know if I have been as nervous before in my career with playing in the Finals for my team because you have no time to miss anything."

She added: "Everything is quick. You have to keep it sweet."

In Reynolds' last time on court, he teamed with Leander Paes to beat Russell and Ross Hutchins 5-2. "Washington broke Springfield's service game twice and wrapped up the set with a Reynolds volley winner to give the Kastles a commanding 15-8 halftime lead," according to the match report.

While Hingis and Anastasia Rodionova won in women's doubles 5-1, the Swiss then teamed up with Paes to get the Kastles a fifth King Trophy and fourth in a row after a 5-4 win in mixed doubles.

"The Kastles tie the mark of four consecutive titles set by Sacramento between 1997-2000. This is also Washington's fifth title in the past six years. or the second year in a row, the Kastles became the first franchise to win all five sets in the Mylan WTT Finals since the league switched to a first to five games format in 1999," according to league statistics.

***

As detailed in this book's introduction, the Kastles claimed a record fifth consecutive title during the league's 40th anniversary. The win tied the Kastles with the Sacramento Capitals run of titles set by the team in 2007.

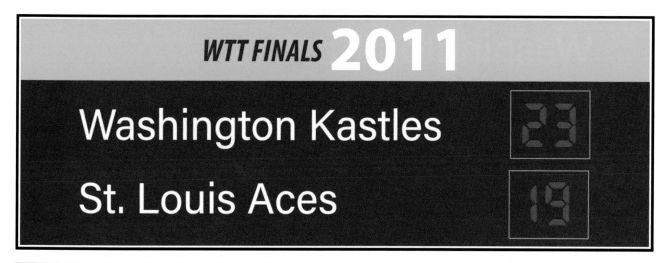

WTT FINALS 2013

| Washington Kastles | |
| Springfield Lasers | |

WTT FINALS 2014

| Washington Kastles | |
| Springfield Lasers | |

WTT FINALS 2015

| Washington Kastles | |
| Austin Aces | |

Chapter Nine: Season Forty-One and Beyond:

The Future

With forty seasons of World TeamTennis completed, executives with the league as well as players both past and present talked about the future of the organization.

Ilana Kloss discussed the future for team tennis in terms of its market share and global growth opportunities. She said that, one day, she sees the league growing into one that doesn't just service tennis communities within the United States, but also around the world.

"I think one of the big goals is really to try to increase the value of every franchise, obviously get more fans to see the product," she said.

Kloss added: "Then I think as it relates to the U.S., we feel right now 10 to 12 teams is probably the best number. We don't want to expand and dilute the player field, so we continue to look at that."

A ball kid waits on-court during a World TeamTennis match. Photo: CameraworkUSA

"We have had many discussions with many countries throughout the world. I think hopefully in the next three to five years you will see the expansion of World TeamTennis to include the rest of the world," said Kloss. "I think that was one of the reasons why it was called 'World TeamTennis' when it started. I think we've focused on the U.S. and obviously have players from all over the world."

The Bryan brothers, two stalwart WTT players over the years, also offered their thoughts on the league's future growth. "I would still like to be involved with WTT. I'd like to see it grow bigger," he said. "This year there were seven teams. I'd like to see that grow to 10, 14, maybe even 20 in the future."

Said Mike Bryan: "Who knows? We might co-own a team, be commissioners. Bobby Jr. and Micaela might be playing. Maybe we'll bring a team to Camarillo, our hometown, and we'd pack it. We want to see it keep growing and getting bigger. It's great now, but there's room for improvement. Hopefully, it can become as big as the NBA."

CoCo Vandeweghe, an up-and-coming American player, also said she hoped to be involved in 40 years. "Hopefully I'll still be involved in some way because I do enjoy it that much," she said. "Hopefully not playing, because I wouldn't want to see my old rickety self out there in 40 years.

Vandeweghe added: "That'd be really tragic. Hopefully I'll be a part of the atmosphere, even if it's from the sidelines."

Chanda Rubin, who's played in the league, said: "I definitely could see it going international. I think so many people now use the Mylan WTT format in different events. I think that internationally, they are very receptive to that style, the atmosphere and having a mix of players on the same team, men and women."

She added: "I'd also love to see it be a part of more grassroots efforts. You have junior WTT. They are understanding the importance of team sports and enjoying playing on a team."

Mary Joe Fernandez, a top player from the U.S. in the past and a tennis commentator, also discussed the league's future, in honor of its 40th anniversary. "I hope that World TeamTennis is played at every level and every state and every region. My children both play tennis and they've played a few events that are with the format of World TeamTennis and they absolutely loved it," she said.

Fernandez continued, "And I think really for the young ones it's so much fun because tennis is tough, it's an individual sport so when you can be part of a team and feel like you are contributing, I think it makes a big difference at an early age."

Rosie Casals, one of the first WTT players and a member of the Original Nine who helped make the WTA Tour a reality, said she hopes the league would continue to expand and become a household name. "To me, I'd like to really see it expand in its timeframe, find a good slot where you're going to get good support from the players and from the fans. You know, make it grow team wise," she said. "We want to see west coast, north, south. I think more teams would be great, and certainly more visibility and exposure, which I think it is starting to get a lot more."

Tracy Austin, another WTT player, shared thoughts mirroring those of Kloss in terms of expansion worldwide for the league. "Well, of course, I'm going to think big time. In 40 years, I'd love to see World TeamTennis all over the world. You know, European teams playing against each other, the United States playing against each other," she said. "And maybe a championship for the world. I think that would be very exciting because people like to watch the men, the women, the mixed, and a team unit, everybody cheering for each other. I hope that World TeamTennis continues for another 40 years."

Zina Garrison, another top U.S. player to take part in the WTT, said, "I would like to see it, first of all, 40 years from now. I just think that every young kid that plays should come through World TeamTennis," she said. "I still like and I remember Billie really kind of explaining World TeamTennis to me, how she would have the older people play, the people that are current and then the young ones learning."

Garrison added, "And I think it's a great concept and I really just hope that the younger kids really take heed of that and have an opportunity to play."

***

In a past interview, Billie Jean King discussed her vision for the league heading well into the 21st century. World TeamTennis, she said, is a welcome part of the tennis world as it doesn't just emphasize the majors, but rather equality, sportsmanship, and, of course, teamwork.

"I think everyone emphasizes the majors so much. In the old days when we played, we emphasized the tour a lot more," she said. "That's when we had over 40 tournaments and TeamTennis in this country when we were doing our best. It really gets back to making sure we have tennis in the community, TeamTennis, Fed Cups, Davis Cups in our communities because it's the only way we're going to get our kids inspired."

Co-founder Billie Jean King gives a young fan a hug. Photo: CameraworkUSA

She added, "I just wish we had more tennis in this country." King also talked about how WTT's recreational league format will continue to grow. "The one great thing about TeamTennis is our format is used in collegiate intramural tennis now, called Tennis on Campus. Our format, I don't know if you realize it, how over the years they're using our TeamTennis format more and more and more in tennis, particularly at the grassroots," she said.

King added: "I think it's really going to help young people get into our sport. I do not think our sport can be big in this country if it isn't a team sport when they sign up to play."

"That's been my mantra forever since I started because I grew up in team sports. I think I understand the psyche of America. I think when children sign up to play, it's got to be in a team," she said. "We have to get rid of the word 'lesson.' I think if you're put on a team as a child like you are in soccer and other sports, I think the children are going to stay in the sport and have more fun if they're on a team."

More importantly for children, and at the very heart of WTT, she said, "They want to play with their friends, learn to compete and have fun."

In 2016, the most recent WTT season, an action-filled 41st year of play saw a new team of champions claim the King Trophy for the very first time. In the changing of the guard after the Kastles' dominance for five consecutive years, the San Diego Aviators beat the Orange County Breakers 25-14 to win their first title. The championship match took place at Forest Hills Stadium at The West Side Tennis Club, which was once the site of the US Open.

Coach John Lloyd, the 2016 Mylan WTT Coach of the Year, spoke highly of his team's win at the historic site. "It brings a lot of memories back; I played back in the US Open when it was on grass and clay," added Lloyd, in his second year at the helm of the new champions. "In fact on this court, I lost to the great Bjorn Borg. It was nice to play on this beautiful court. To come back and win this title was great."

The San Diego Aviators captured their first WTT title with a 25-14 victory over the Orange County Breakers. The 2016 championship match was held at Forest Hills Stadium in Forest Hills, N.Y., the former home of the US Open. Pictured (l. to r. – back row): Darija Jurak, Shelby Rogers, WTT co-founder Billie Jean King, WTT CEO/Commissioner Ilana Kloss, and Coach John Lloyd; (l. to r. – front row): Ryan Harrison and Finals MVP Raven Klaasen. Photo: CameraworkUSA

Chapter Ten: Fun Facts from 40 Years of WTT

At its core, World TeamTennis was created to provide a competitive and, of course, uniquely entertaining facet of the sport for fans to enjoy around the world. It's no surprise, then, that the players themselves have had some pretty crazy experiences over the years that expand far beyond the multi-colored courts on which they play each season.

Here is a collection of just a fraction of those moments from some of the fan favorites over the last 40 years:

Kim Clijsters played for the St. Louis Aces and the New York Sportimes. Photo: Danny Riese

Kim Clijsters:

In 2009, Clijsters thought she left a custom mouthpiece on a plate in the players' lounge and that it had been thrown away. And what happens when a major champion loses something near and dear? Well, all the staff of the St. Louis Aces team, including the trainer from the Springfield Lasers go digging. Trash bags were torn apart and even a few interns from the St. Louis franchise jumped into a dumpster to look. It turns out, however, that Clijsters found the item in her pocket. But Clijsters, as she was known on the WTA Tour, was said to have been extremely nice and charming during the whole episode, so no one much cared.

Lindsay Davenport:

"I keep going back to my 1997 year. We had to get from two cities in the Midwest. Somebody, who I won't say, woke up really late, so we ended up getting off to a late start and we had a match that night. We're all in a van and going way too fast, so, of course, our coach Scott Davis gets pulled over. And because we were going so fast, they actually handcuffed him and pulled him out of the car and put him into the police car behind us. Richey Reneberg and Brian MacPhie were laughing so hard and started taking pictures, to which the cop then came running back to the car to cuff them. We were on the highway somewhere in the middle of Missouri for a good hour before we talked our way out of it. We pulled into Springfield at 6:55 and barely made the match. All of us were crying laughing the whole way."

Lindsay Davenport claimed three World TeamTennis titles with the Sacramento Capitals in 1997, 1998 and 2007. Photo: Bill Putnam

Ramon Delgado:

There's many a time when a World TeamTennis player becomes some of a hometown hero for their franchise. That was the case for Ramon Delgado when he played for the Newport Beach Breakers in 2006. In fact, he had a fan club that called themselves the Desperate Housewives for Ramon Delgado, a play off the popular reality television program *Desperate Housewives*.

Mary Joe Fernandez:

"You know what the best part was? That, as a team, you would travel at night sometimes and go play in the morning and we would become a family and we would play pranks on each other. So we would always be so scared if we were in the bus or on the plane and we'd fall asleep, as someone would be tying your shoelaces together or they would be painting with a magic marker on your face. So, you're always kind of on edge. And I never went to college, so that was sort of my college experience, being with my group on a day-to-day basis and really having so much fun. It's great memories and I love still watching it today."

Zina Garrison:

"One of my favorite stories probably was with Kathy Rinaldi and we were getting ready to go play in Springfield, Missouri and I don't like to fly, a lot of people know that. We were getting ready to fly and we overheard one of the people say that it was bad weather. So, I asked the flight attendant is 'everything going to be okay?' And she goes, 'Oh, I hope so. This is my first trip.' And I just freaked out and I said to Trevor Kronemann, 'Can we please get off the flight and drive?' So I always remember that team with Kathy Rinaldi and Trevor Kronemann and the fact that we all jelled together. They were willing to get off the plane and go with me just to be part of a team."

Nicole Gibbs:

"One night last year, we opted to travel after our match rather than the following morning, which we thought was genius because it would give us a day off when we got to the next destination. Little did we know that we would be so exhausted when we got to the next destination that we were pretty much useless the next day. I remember getting off the private jet, which we were lucky enough to take, and we were in a van to the hotel and everybody was just so punch-drunk Everybody was kind of cracking jokes that were not funny at all and we were just dying laughing. That was definitely one of my favorite experiences."

Madison Keys:

"One weekend when Venus was there, I didn't realize that she had a dog. Her bag started moving and I was hearing things. I was convinced that her bag was possessed or something. And out popped Harold. That is how I met Harold for the first time."

Raven Klaasen:

"I'm from South Africa and I kind of come from a family that likes to dance and likes to have fun. Last year, halfway through the season, there was a song playing in the crowd and our DJ saw a couple of people dancing and all of a sudden it was a dance that all of the young kids knew. At the end of the match, I was sort of like, 'Hey guys, can one of you come down to teach me that?' So the guys came down to the court and we got some videos and they were teaching me the song. For the rest of the season, we ended up doing that at halftime with me getting out with some kids. I thought that was really fun to interact with the kids and to have them watch tennis. I really enjoyed that and hopefully we get to do some more."

Alla Kudryavtseva:

"It was actually the toughest moment for us as a team off the court. We had to leave, I believe it was Springfield, and fly over to Philadelphia. We finished the match at around 11pm and got up to go to the airport around 3am. After finishing a match, you can't fall asleep for a couple of hours because the adrenaline is running. When we met in the lobby, it was so much. Jarmere Jenkins would just fall asleep anywhere he sat down, sometimes without even sitting down. Nicole Gibbs was groggy and slow. Teymur Gabashvili acted like nothing happened. Teymur acted like he had just eight hours of sleep and was just fine. It's a very irritable moment when you have to do that as a tennis player, when you don't sleep and have to go to the airport. It's frustrating and all you want to do is chill out and relax. [It was great] just how nice everybody was to each other and how supportive and helpful and accommodating. It shows what kind of people you're with when under stressful situations and lack of sleep and lack of rest, you can still be nice to each other. We have a picture where the four of us are sharing a row in the airplane commercial flight and we're just sleeping on each other. It's so cute. I love that picture of us. The best picture I think we have."

Martina Navratilova:

"We missed the French (Open) and didn't care. We were really on the road quite a bit. I've never been so tired in my life. That's when I learned to sleep on airplanes, cause you had to, otherwise you were going to die."

Andy Roddick:

"It's funny; the rewarding parts are probably the challenging parts. Every single person who has ever played World TeamTennis says the travel's tough. But then you look back at seasons from 10 years ago and you're going, 'Wasn't that fun when we couldn't get good food and we were all beat up?' It's one of those things that gets better with age."

Andy Roddick played for his hometown Austin Aces in 2014. Photo: CameraworkUSA

Anastasia Rodionova:

"Usually whatever happens with the Kastles, stays with the Kastles. We do have quite a few interesting stories, but I don't know if some of them we should share. For example, last year we had to drive quite a bit from the hotel to the venue or from one city to another. For some reason, Murphy kept saying for all three weeks, 'Don't get T-Boned during the season!' He didn't care if we got T-boned after the season, the most important thing for him was 'don't get T-boned during the season.'"

CoCo Vandeweghe:

"We played a credit card game when I was playing for the Orange County Breakers [in 2013]. It was my last match of the season, so we all decided we would throw our credit cards in and have the waitress pull one out of a hat. Unfortunately, I didn't win, but my teammate Maria Elena lost and had to pay for everyone. It was like a $400 bill."

Venus Williams:

"When you play on a team, you have to wear the team colors. There was a match when my skirt went missing. I put it on the table and I couldn't find it. So, the match is about to start and I'm like, 'It's fine. I'll put on some undershorts. I don't care.' It turns out the coach's fiancée picked up the skirt. She just kept picking up after Murphy because she says he loses everything. We were in a major panic with what I was going to wear!"

Venus Williams celebrates the 2012 WTT Championship title in Charleston, S.C., with her Washington Kastles teammates – coach Murphy Jensen, Arina Rodionova, owner Mark Ein, Leander Paes and Anastasia Rodionova. Photo: CameraworkUSA

WTT Championship Teams from the League's History

YEAR	LOCATION	CHAMPIONSHIP
2016	Forest Hills, N.Y.	San Diego Aviators def. Orange County Breakers 25-14
2015	Washington, D.C.	Washington Kastles def. Austin Aces 24-18
2014	Springfield, Mo.	Washington Kastles def. Springfield Lasers 25-13
2013	Washington, D.C.	Washington Kastles def. Springfield Lasers 25-12
2012	Charleston, S.C.	Washington Kastles def. Sacramento Capitals 20-19
2011	Charleston, S.C.	Washington Kastles def. St. Louis Aces 23-19
2010	Kansas City, Mo.	Kansas City Explorers def. New York Sportimes 21-18
2009	Washington, D.C.	Washington Kastles def. Springfield Lasers 23-20
2008	Sacramento, Calif.	New York Buzz def. Kansas City Explorers 21-18
2007	Sacramento, Calif.	Sacramento Capitals def. New York Buzz 24-20
2006	Newport Beach, Calif.	Philadelphia Freedoms def. Newport Beach Breakers 21-14
2005	Sacramento, Calif.	New York Sportimes def. Newport Beach Breakers 21-18
2004	Flushing Meadows, N.Y.	Newport Beach Breakers def. Delaware Smash 23-17
2003	Flushing Meadows, N.Y.	Delaware Smash def. Sacramento Capitals 21-14
2002	Flushing Meadows, N.Y.	Sacramento Capitals def. New York Buzz 21-13
2001	Flushing Meadows, N.Y.	Philadelphia Freedoms def. Springfield Lasers 20-18
2000	Flushing Meadows, N.Y.	Sacramento Capitals def. Delaware Smash 21-20
1999	Sacramento, Calif.	Sacramento Capitals def. Springfield Lasers 23-15
1998	Sacramento, Calif.	Sacramento Capitals def. New York OTBzz 30-13
1997	Orlando, Fla.	Sacramento Capitals won title based on regular season record (finals rained out)
1996	Wesley Chapel, Fla.	St. Louis Aces def. Delaware Smash 27-16
1995	Charlotte, N.C.	New Jersey Stars def. Atlanta Thunder 28-20
1994	Sacramento, Calif.	New Jersey Stars def. Idaho Sneakers 28-25
1993	Atlanta, Ga.	Wichita Advantage def. Newport Beach Dukes 26-23
1992	Atlanta, Ga.	Atlanta Thunder def. Newport Beach Dukes 30-17
1991	Atlanta, Ga.	Atlanta Thunder def. Los Angeles Strings 27-16
1990	Los Angeles, Calif.	Los Angeles Strings def. Raleigh Edge 27-16
1989	Sacramento, Calif.	San Antonio Racquets def. Sacramento Capitals 27-25
1988	Charlotte, N.C.	Charlotte Heat def. New Jersey Stars 27-22
1987	Charlotte, N.C.	Charlotte Heat def. San Antonio Racquets 25-20
1986	San Antonio, Texas	San Antonio Racquets def. Sacramento Capitals 25-23
1985	San Antonio, Texas	San Diego Buds def. St. Louis Slims 25-24
1984	Los Angeles, Calif.	San Diego Buds - Season Consisted of One-Week Tournament
1983	Los Angeles, Calif.	Chicago Fyre def. Los Angeles Strings 26-20
1982		Dallas Stars def. Phoenix Sunsets 27-22
1981		Los Angeles Strings - Champion Determined by Regular Season Record

1979-80	League Hiatus	
1978	Los Angeles/Boston	Los Angeles Strings def. Boston Lobsters 108-93 (24-21, 30-20, 26-27, 28-25)*
1977	New York/Phoenix, Ariz.	New York Apples def. Phoenix Racquets 55-39 (27-22, 28-17)*
1976	New York/San Francisco	New York Sets def. San Francisco Golden Gaters 91-57 (31-23, 29-21, 31-13)*
1975	Pittsburgh/San Francisco	Pittsburgh Triangles def. San Francisco Golden Gaters 74-65 (25-26, 28-25, 21-14)*
1974	Denver/Philadelphia	Denver Racquets def. Philadelphia Freedoms 55-48 (27-21, 28-24)*

THE DENVER RACQUETS

The Denver Racquets made history as the first World TeamTennis champions in 1974. Pictured (l. to r.) Cliff Buchholz, Francoise Durr, Jeff Austin, Pam Austin, player/coach Tony Roche, Kristien Kemmer Shaw, Andrew Pattison, Stephanie Johnson, trainer Lloyd Williams and team mascot Topspin. Photo: World TeamTennis

1984 WTT Champions - San Diego Buds: (l. to r.) Brad Gilbert,
Andrea Leand, Pam Teeguarden and Ross Case.

1988 WTT Champions – Charlotte Heat: (l. to r.) Eddie Edwards, Elna Reinach,
Tim Wilkison, Monica Reinach and coach Karl Coombes.

1991 WTT Champions - Atlanta Thunder: (l. to r.) Kelly Evernden, Jennifer Capriati, Mariaan de Swardt, coach Craig Kardon and Marty Davis. Martina Navratilova (not pictured).

1992 WTT Champions - Atlanta Thunder: (l. to r.) WTT co-founder Billie Jean King with team members including Brett Steven, coach Craig Kardon, Kelly Evernden, Martina Navratilova and Heather Ludloff.

1993 WTT Champions - Wichita Advantage (back row) - Buff Farrow, coach Mervyn Webster, T.J. Middleton; (front row) Julie Steven, Lori McNeil.

1994 WTT Champions - New Jersey Stars: (l. to r.) John-Laffnie de Jager, Mariaan de Swardt, coach Craig Kardon, Martina Navratilova and Brian Devening.

1997 WTT Champions - Sacramento Capitals: (l. to r.) Owner Ramey Osborne, Lindsay Davenport, Kristine Kunce, Richey Reneberg, Brian MacPhie, Corina Morariu and player/coach Scott Davis.

2001 WTT Champions - Philadelphia Freedoms: (l. to r.) Lisa Raymond, David Di Lucia, Don Johnson, Rennae Stubbs, coach Raja Chaudhuri, general manager Jeff Harrison, team owner Billie Jean King and WTT CEO/Commissioner Ilana Kloss.

2002 WTT Champions - Sacramento Capitals (l. to r.) - Brian MacPhie, Ashley Harkleroad, Mark Knowles, Coach Wayne Bryan and Elena Likhovtseva. Photo: CameraworkUSA

2003 WTT Champions – Delaware Smash: (l. to r.) Samantha Reeves, Paul Goldstein, coach Brad Dancer, Scott Humphries and Liezel Huber.

2004 WTT Champions – Newport Beach Breakers: (l. to r.) WTT co-founder Billie Jean King, Aniko Kapros, Ellis Ferreira, Coach Dick Leach, Ramon Delgado and Nana Miyagi. Photo: CameraworkUSA

2005 WTT Champions – New York Sportimes: (front) Jenny Hopkins, Rajeev Ram, Martina Hingis and Jeff Morrison. Back row: Advanta representative Peter Fishbach, Sportimes staff Dan Beccaria, WTT co-founders Larry King and Billie Jean King, and Sportimes owner Claude Okin. Photo: CameraworkUSA

2006 WTT Champions – Philadelphia Freedoms: (l. to r.) Rennae Stubbs, Coach Craig Kardon, Jaymon Crabb, Lisa Raymond and Daniel Nestor. Photo: CameraworkUSA

2010 WTT Champions – Kansas City Explorers: (l. to r.) Sam Groth, Jarmila Groth, Kveta Peschke, Ricardo Mello and Coach Brent Haygarth (back). Photo: CameraworkUSA

2011 WTT Champions – Washington Kastles: (l. to r.) Bobby Reynolds, Rennae Stubbs, Coach Murphy Jensen, Arina Rodionova and Leander Paes. Photo: CameraworkUSA

2012 WTT Champions – Washington Kastles: (l. to r.) Coach Murphy Jensen, Anastasia Rodionova, Venus Williams, Bobby Reynolds, Leander Paes and Arina Rodionova. Photo: CameraworkUSA

2013 WTT Champions – Washington Kastles: (l. to r.) Coach Murphy Jensen, Martina Hingis,
Bobby Reynolds, Anastasia Rodionova and Leander Paes. Photo: CameraworkUSA

League Innovations and Firsts

WTT has historically been a league of firsts and innovations, many of which have been implemented in the professional WTA and ATP tours.

Along with its commitment to equality for prize money and for men and women being treated the same, WTT is also responsible for the following:

Martina Hingis and Anastasia Rodionova being coached by Murphy Jensen of the Washington Kastles. Photo: CameraworkUSA

- Professional sports league where men and women have equal roles.
- In 2015, the league introduced an on-court service clock which counts down 25 seconds from the end of a point to the next serve. The first time violation per set is a warning and additional violations will result in point penalties.
- Pro tennis competition to regularly feature no-ad scoring – first to four points wins the game.
- Features on-court coaching.
- Mylan WTT encourages fan participation. Mylan WTT crowds are encouraged to be vocal about great play (while still being respectful of all players) and are allowed to enter/exit the stadium during play without having to wait for a changeover. Often between games, music is played or a DJ fires up the crowd.

- Let serves are played.
- Sets are played to five games (nine-point tiebreak played at 4-4).
- Invented the use of Supertiebreaker and Extended Play in tennis.
- Tennis fans are allowed to keep balls hit out of play and get them autographed after the match.
- Substitutions are allowed during a Mylan WTT match.
- Mylan WTT matches have half-times, Extended Play and Supertiebreakers.
- Player names on the back of shirts.
- Played on multi-colored courts.
- Use of instant replay technology in 2005 with the Coaches Challenge.
- Similarly as with other professional league team sports, the use of timeouts during match play was added in 2012. Each team is allotted two timeouts per set with an additional timeout being awarded to each team if a match goes into Extended Play. Timeouts will be twenty (:20) seconds in length and do not carry over between sets. Only the coach may call a timeout. Coaches or players may enter the court area during these breaks in action.

World TeamTennis' signature, multi-colored courts on display. Photo: CameraworkUSA

The league also achieved the following milestones as detailed in the book and on its web site, including:

2015: TURNING 40 – World TeamTennis becomes only the fifth U.S. pro sports league to reach the 40th season milestone, joining the National Football League, National Basketball Association, National Hockey League and Major League Baseball.

World TeamTennis co-founders Billie Jean King and Larry King at the 40th season celebration in March 2015 in Indian Wells, Calif. Photo: CameraworkUSA

2011-2015: THE KASTLES ERA –

» In 2011, the Washington Kastles completed the first undefeated season in WTT history (16-0), and won their 2nd WTT Championship with a victory over St. Louis Aces.

» One year later, the Kastles did it again. Led by Venus Williams, Washington edged Sacramento in the 2012 Finals to complete their second undefeated season and hoist the King Trophy for the third time in franchise history.

» Before winning their 3rd consecutive and 4th overall championship in 2013, the Kastles became the first league champion to be invited to the White House to meet with the President.

» Washington also rewrote the sports record books during the 2013 season by setting the mark of 34 consecutive wins (2011-2013), the longest streak in major pro sports league history. The previous mark of 33 consecutive wins was held by the NBA's 1971-72 Lakers.

• In 2015, the Kastles set a league record of five consecutive championship titles (2011-15) surpassing the record they shared with the Sacramento Capitals (1997-2000).

The Washington Kastles rewrite sports history set the major U.S. pro sports league mark for most consecutive victories at 34 (2011-2013) – breaking the previous record set by the NBA's Los Angeles Lakers. Pictured (l. to r.): Leander Paes, Anastasia Rodionova, Bobby Reynolds, owner Mark Ein, Martina Hingis, Kevin Anderson and coach Murphy Jensen. Photo: Willis Bretz

2013: NEW PARTNERS - Mylan, one of the world's leading generics and specialty pharmaceutical companies, and World TeamTennis announced a three-year agreement whereby Mylan will serve as the title sponsor of WTT, which was renamed Mylan World TeamTennis beginning in 2013. Andy Roddick and Venus Williams join the World TeamTennis ownership group in May 2013.

2009: NAVRATILOVA TURNS 20 - Martina Navratilova, playing for the Boston Lobsters in 2009, becomes first player to play 20 seasons in WTT. Kim Clijsters comes out of retirement and makes her WTT debut for St. Louis in July 2009. Less than two months later, she returns to the pro tour and stuns the sports world by winning the US Open title.

Commissioner Ilana Kloss recognizes Martina Navratilova for her record
20th World TeamTennis season in 2009. Photo: CameraworkUSA

2005: GRAF, HINGIS HIGHLIGHT 30ᵗʰ SEASON - WTT celebrates its 30ᵗʰ anniversary and introduces Instant replay to professional tennis competition. Stefanie Graf makes her return to pro tennis for the first time since 1999 to play WTT. Martina Hingis makes her WTT debut and leads the New York Sportimes to their first title. Hingis lost only one set during the 2005 season and was named MVP of the WTT Finals. Her WTT performance spurred the tennis great to make a successful return to the WTA Tour.

**Martina Hingis and John McEnroe playing mixed doubles together
for the New York Sportimes. Photo: World TeamTennis**

2002: AMBASSADOR AGASSI - Andre Agassi joined WTT as a player and League ambassador.

2000: 4-PEAT & ANDY IS A HIT - Sacramento had an unprecedented four-peat, winning the title from 1997 to 2000. Seven years later, the Capitals becomes the first team in WTT history to win six championships with the 2007 title. A 17-year-old Andy Roddick breaks onto the pro scene and makes his WTT debut playing a full season for the Idaho Sneakers.

1992: A NEW NAME - In line with the growing global popularity of the sport, the professional league is rebranded from TeamTennis to World TeamTennis.

1990: LEGENDS SIGN ON – Current Mylan WTT CEO/Commissioner Ilana Kloss signs Jimmy Connors and Martina Navratilova to the League's first multi-year marquee player contracts.

In 1990, Ilana Kloss signs Martina Navratilova and Jimmy Connors to the first multi-year marquee contracts. Photo: World TeamTennis

1984: COMMISSIONER KING - Billie Jean King becomes the first woman commissioner in pro sports history.

1981: TEAMTENNIS - Following a brief hiatus, the league returns as TeamTennis.

Los Angeles Strings owner Jerry Buss celebrates the 1978 WTT title with two of his star players – Chris Evert and Ilie Nastase. Photo: World TeamTennis

1974: FIRST SET – World TeamTennis, which was founded by Billie Jean King, Larry King, Fred Barman, Jordon Kaiser, Dennis Murphy and Frank Fuhrer, debuts as the inaugural season introduces professional team tennis competition to the sports landscape.

» Based on a concept of gender equity, WTT is also the first professional sports league to feature men and women on the same team. It is also the debut of WTT's unique multi-colored court.
» The Denver Racquets defeat the Philadelphia Freedoms to win the first championship.
» League co-founder Billie Jean King is named as the League's first MVP and is also the first woman to coach a team with male pros as the player-coach of the Freedoms.
» Among the first team owners was the Los Angeles Strings' Jerry Buss, who went on to own the NBA's Los Angeles Lakers. His daughter Jeanie became the team GM in 1981. Robert Kraft, current owner of the NFL's New England Patriots, became owner of the Boston Lobsters in 1975.
» On May 6, 1974, the first World TeamTennis match was played when the Philadelphia Freedoms hosted the Pittsburgh Triangles at the Spectrum. Philadelphia won 31-25.
» On May 9, 1974, WTT becomes the first regularly scheduled tennis serves coverage on HBO when the New York Sets take on the Pittsburgh Triangles.

World TeamTennis Awards (1974-2016)

MOST VALUABLE PLAYER

2016:
Most Valuable Player
Female – Nicole Gibbs (Orange County Breakers)
Male – Ryan Harrison (San Diego Aviators)

2015
Female (co-MVP) – Anabel Medina Garrigues (California Dream)
Female (co-MVP) – Anastasia Rodionova (Washington Kastles)
Male – Teymuraz Gabashvili (Austin Aces)

2014
Female – Daniela Hantuchova (San Diego Aviators)
Male – Marcelo Melo (Philadelphia Freedoms)

2013
Female – Martina Hingis (Washington Kastles)
Male – Jean-Julien Rojer (Springfield Lasers)

2012
Female – Martina Hingis (New York Sportimes)
Male – Bobby Reynolds (Washington Kastles)

2011
Female – Liezel Huber (St. Louis Aces)
Male – Leander Paes (Washington Kastles)

2010
Female – Lindsay Davenport (St. Louis Aces)
Male – Martin Damm (Springfield Lasers)

2009
Female – Vania King (Springfield Lasers)
Male – Leander Paes (Washington Kastles)

2008
Female – Rennae Stubbs (Kansas City Explorers)
Male – Ramon Delgado (Newport Beach Breakers)

2007
Female – Tamarine Tanasugarn (Springfield Lasers)
Male – Mark Knowles (Sacramento Capitals)

2006
Female – Angela Haynes (Delaware Smash)
Male – Daniel Nestor (Philadelphia Freedoms)

2005
Female – Elena Likhovtseva (Sacramento Capitals)
Male – Mark Knowles (Sacramento Capitals)

2004
Female – Nicole Vaidisova (Sacramento Capitals)
Male – Dimitry Tursunov (Sacramento Capitals)

2003
Female – Samantha Reeves (Delaware Smash)
Male – Paul Goldstein (Delaware Smash)

2002
Female – Katarina Srebotnik (New York Hamptons)
Male – Mahesh Bhupathi (New York Buzz)

2001
Female – Lisa Raymond (Philadelphia Freedoms)
Male – Mark Knowles (Sacramento Capitals)

2000
Female – Mariaan de Swardt (Delaware Smash)
Male – Richey Reneberg (Sacramento Capitals)

1999
Female – Elena Tatarkova (Springfield Lasers)
Male – Grant Stafford (Springfield Lasers)

1998
Female – Larisa Neiland (Springfield Lasers)
Male – Brian MacPhie (Sacramento Capitals)

1997
Female – Lindsay Davenport (Sacramento Capitals)
Male – Brian MacPhie (Sacramento Capitals)

1996
Female – Lisa Raymond (St. Louis Aces)
Male – Brian MacPhie (Sacramento Capitals)

1995
Female – Amy Frazier (Idaho Sneakers)
Male – Brett Hansen-Dent (Idaho Sneakers)

1994
Female – Larisa Neiland (Newport Beach Dukes)
Male – Kelly Jones (Newport Beach Dukes)

1993
Female – Martina Navratilova (Atlanta Thunder)
Male – Jimmy Connors (Phoenix Smash) & Trevor Kronemann (Newport Beach Dukes)

1992
Female – Martina Navratilova (Atlanta Thunder)
Male – Mikael Pernfors (Tampa Bay Action)

1991
Female – Martina Navratilova (Atlanta Thunder)
Male – Sammy Giammalva (San Antonio Racquets)

1990
Female – Robin White (Los Angeles Strings)
Male – Trevor Kronemann (Charlotte Heat)

1989
Female – Ronnie Reis (Portland Panthers)
Male – Robert Van't Hof (Sacramento Capitals)

1988
Female – Elna Reinach (Charlotte Heat)
Male – Blaine Willenborg (South Florida Breakers)

1987
Female – Elna Reinach (Charlotte Heat)
Male – Kim Warwick (San Antonio Racquets)

1986
Female – Pam Casale (Sacramento Capitals)
Male – Kim Warwick (San Antonio Racquets)

1985
Female – Mary Lou Piatek (San Diego Buds)
Male – Butch Waltz (San Diego Buds)

1978
Female – Martina Navratilova (Boston Lobsters)
Male – Frew McMillan (San Francisco Golden Gaters)

1977
Female – Chris Evert (Phoenix Racquets)
Male – Frew McMillan (San Francisco Golden Gaters)

1976
Female – Chris Evert (Phoenix Racquets)
Male – Sandy Mayer (New York Sets)

1975
Female – Evonne Goolagong (Pittsburgh Triangles)
Male – Tom Okker (San Francisco Golden Gaters)

1974
Billie Jean King (Philadelphia Freedoms)

ROOKIE OF THE YEAR

2016
Female - Michaella Krajicek (Springfield Lasers)
Male - Fabrice Martin (Philadelphia Freedoms)

2015
Female – Alla Kudryavtseva (Austin Aces)
Male – Neal Skupski (California Dream)

2014
Female – Anabel Medina Garrigues (Texas Wild)
Male – Somdev Devvarman (San Diego Aviators)

2013
Female – Alisa Kleybanova (Springfield Lasers)
Male – Steve Johnson (Orange County Breakers)

2012
Female – Kristyna Pliskova (Philadelphia Freedoms)
Male – John-Patrick Smith (Orange County Breakers)

2011
Female – Arina Rodionova (Washington Kastles)
Male – Jean-Julien Rojer (St. Louis Aces)

2010
Female – Courtney Nagle (Philadelphia Freedoms)
Male – Bobby Reynolds (Washington Kastles)

2009
Female – Liga Dekmeijere (St. Louis Aces)
Male – Michael Russell (Kansas City Explorers)

2008
Female – Yaroslava Shvedova (New York Buzz)
Male – Travis Parrott (Philadelphia Freedoms)

2007
Female – Jarmila Gajdosova (Kansas City Explorers)
Male – Jesse Witten (New York Sportimes)

2006
Female – Victoria Azarenka (Springfield Lasers)
Male – David Martin (New York Sportimes)

2005
Female – Katerina Bondarenko (Newport Beach Breakers)
Male – Rik de Voest (Springfield Lasers)

2004
Female – Nicole Vaidisova (Sacramento Capitals)
Male – Dimitry Tursunov (Sacramento Capitals)

2003
Female – Bea Bielik (New York Sportimes)
Male – Daniel Nestor (Sacramento Capitals)

2002
Female – Samantha Reeves (Delaware Smash)
Male – Scott Humphries (Delaware Smash)

2001
Female – Anastasia Myskina (Springfield Lasers)
Male – Mark Knowles (Sacramento Capitals)

2000
Female – Lina Krasnoroutskaya (Springfield Lasers)
Male – James Blake (Hartford FoxForce)

1999
Female – Elena Tatarkova (Springfield Lasers)
Male – Grant Stafford (Springfield Lasers)

1998
Female – Nana Miyagi (New York OTBzz)
Male – Geoff Grant (New York OTBzz)

1997
Female – Mary Joe Fernandez (Kansas City Explorers)
Male – Richey Reneberg (Sacramento Capitals)

1996
Female – Lisa Raymond (St. Louis Aces)
Male – Brian MacPhie (Sacramento Capitals)

1995
Female – Brenda Schultz-McCarthy (New York OTBzz)
Male – Brett Hansen-Dent (Idaho Sneakers)

1994
Female – Larisa Neiland (Newport Beach Dukes)
Male – Sandon Stolle (Sacramento Capitals)

1993
Female – Lindsay Davenport (Sacramento Capitals)
Male – Mats Wilander (New Jersey Stars)

1992
Female – Patty Fendick (Sacramento Capitals)
Male – Mikael Pernfors (Tampa Bay Action)

1991
Female – Ginger Helgeson (Charlotte Heat)
Male – Jimmy Connors (Los Angeles Strings)

1990
Female – Amy Frazier (Newport Beach Dukes)
Male – Trevor Kronemann (Charlotte Heat)

1989
Female – Ronnie Reis (Portland Panthers)
Male – Jean Fleurian (Fresno Sun Nets)

1988
Female – Heather Ludloff (South Florida Breakers)
Male – Blaine Willenborg (South Florida Breakers)

1987
Female – Elna Reinach (Charlotte Heat)
Male – Eric Korita (San Antonio Racquets)

1986
Female – Pam Casale (Sacramento Capitals)
Male – Mike DePalmer (Oakland Aces)

1985
Robin White (San Diego Buds)

1977
Male – Bjorn Borg (Cleveland Nets)
Female – Sue Barker (Indiana Loves)

1976
Male – Rod Laver (San Diego Friars)
Female – Chris Evert (Phoenix Racquets)

1975
Male – Marty Riessen (Cleveland Nets)
Female – Greer Stevens (Boston Lobsters)

COACH OF THE YEAR

2016	John Lloyd (San Diego Aviators)
2015	Rick Leach (Austin Aces)
2014	David Macpherson (San Diego Aviators)
2013	Murphy Jensen (Washington Kastles)
2012	Murphy Jensen (Washington Kastles)
2011	Murphy Jensen (Washington Kastles)
2010	John-Laffnie "JL" de Jager (Springfield Lasers)
2009	John-Laffnie "JL" de Jager (Springfield Lasers)
2008	Brent Haygarth (Kansas City Explorers)
2007	John-Laffnie "JL" de Jager (Springfield Lasers)
2006	Wayne Bryan (Sacramento Capitals)
2005	Wayne Bryan (Sacramento Capitals)
2004	Wayne Bryan (Sacramento Capitals)
2003	Brad Dancer (Delaware Smash)
2002	Eric Kutner (New York Buzz)
2001	Raja Chaudhuri (Philadelphia Freedoms)
2000	Kevin Forbes (Sacramento Capitals)
1999	Ken Goodall (Springfield Lasers)
1998	Inderjit Singh (New York OTBzz)
1997	Scott Davis (Sacramento Capitals)
1996	Rick Flach (St. Louis Aces)
1995	Greg Patton (Idaho Sneakers)
1994	Angel Lopez (Newport Beach Dukes)
1993	Greg Patton (Newport Beach Dukes)
1992	Craig Kardon (Atlanta Thunder)
1991	Bob McKinley (San Antonio Racquets)
1990	John Lloyd (Los Angeles Strings)
1989	Asim Sengun (New Jersey Stars)
1983	Ilana Kloss (Chicago Fyre)
1977	Fred Stolle (New York Apples)
1976	Fred Stolle (New York Sets)
1975	Frew McMillan (San Francisco Golden Gaters)
1974	Tony Roche (Denver Racquets)

Acknowledgements

The opportunity to write World TeamTennis' history has been a dream come true for a tennis player who grew up in Forest Hills, Queens, the home of the US Open. I grew up playing the sport and would religiously watch any and all tennis matches I could see.

As I learned more about tennis, I learned about Billie Jean King's efforts to spread equality through sport. Her message has stuck with me to this day, especially the mantra, "Pressure is a privilege."

The ability to read the history of this league, too, has been awe-inspiring. The lives it has touched, including the players, the executives, and the fans, is simply astounding. I firmly believe that World TeamTennis has made the world a better place, opening the eyes and minds of children everywhere about the beauty that tennis has to offer personally, professionally, and otherwise.

The chance to have countless conversations with individuals involved in WTT has been a long and rewarding process, too. I would like to thank those who took the time to speak with me about their involvement, including, of course, Billie Jean King and Ilana Kloss. Over the years, and ever since interning for WTT, Billie and Ilana have been two of my biggest supporters as I've followed my dreams of writing about tennis and as a journalist.

I would also like to thank Rosie Crews of WTT for her support throughout the process, as well as the rest of the WTT staff, such as Samantha Shaw, Jason Spitz, Delaine Mast, Elaine Wingfield, Matt Fitzgerald, Natalee Jarrett, Nancy Falconer, Tip Nunn, Diane Stone, and others who so selflessly work on making the league the best it can be.

As I mentioned, I had the ability to speak with some of the greatest contributors to tennis. I would like to thank these people for their time, including Larry King, Chris Evert, Mark Ein, Lorne Abony, David Macpherson, John-Laffnie de Jager, Glenn Arrington, Anna-Lena Groenefeld, Jan-Michael Gambill, Michael Russell, Mike Bryan, Katrina Adams, Rick Leach, Taylor Townsend, Murphy Jensen, Josh Cohen, John Lloyd, Jen Smith, Valerie McCutchen, Brian MacPhie, Kim Reser, Bob Belote, Tom Adams, Jodie Adams, Isaac Leamer, Kerry Schneider, and countless others.

Of course, none of this would have been possible without my family, friends and mentors. I'd like to thank my mother, Nancy Snyder, for always supporting me in whatever I set my mind to, as well as my father, Jonathan Snyder, for introducing me to tennis, as well as my step-mother, Rachel Pratt, for her advice and guidance.

I would also like to thank my uncle Jonathan Cooper for inspiring in me a passion for tennis from an early age. My times attending the US Open with him are some of my happiest memories from childhood. I'm so glad it's a tradition we've kept going ever since.

I would also like to thank my brother and sister, August and Genevieve, for inspiring in me a confidence in my writing and a love of life through the eyes of two of the most awesome kids around. It's an honor to be your older brother.

To my grandparents Cevia Rosol, George Rosol, Marcia Snyder, Karen Cooper, and Arthur Cooper, thank you for helping to raise me and inspiring in me the ability to follow my dreams and be the best version of myself in everything I do.

My friends have been my rock through this process, including my former tennis team captain and photographer friend Billie Weiss, as well as my other friends who let me talk their ears off about the writing process, including Samantha Hoffmann, Ariel Brodsky, Marley Witham, Grace Pastore, Alex Forney, and Shalene Gupta. I also want to thank my tennis team at Goucher College and members of *The Quindecim*, the student newspaper, and the faculty at Columbia University's Graduate School of Journalism for teaching me the tricks of the trade.

I wouldn't be where I am today without my journalism and writing mentors. Thank you to David Zurawik, Mary Marchand, Nsenga Burton, Andrew Nusca, Scott Olster, JP Mangalindan, and Ilsa Cowen.

Tennis really is a metaphor for life. I invite you to catch the next WTT match you can and take every opportunity to pick up a tennis racquet, grab a can of tennis balls, and play.

Sincerely,
Benjamin Snyder / author